A GUIDED TOUR OF DUBLIN

Anna Livia—Keystone on Custom House,
symbolizing the Liffey.

A Guided Tour of Dublin

by

Charlotte Bielenberg

Illustrated by Roland Pym

THE MERCIER PRESS
4 BRIDGE ST., CORK

SBN 85342 035 1

Printed in Great Britain
Computer Filmset
By C. Tinling and Co. Ltd.
Prescot and London

Acknowledgements

The extract from 'Dublin' is reprinted by permission
of Faber and Faber Ltd., from *The Collected Poems of
Louis MacNeice*. Grateful acknowledgement is made
to Mr M. B. Yeats for permission to quote from the
works of W. B. Yeats.

Contents

Foreword

The idea of writing this book about Dublin came to me when out of several tours this particular combination of places proved the most successful in all my experience as a Dublin guide. I am well aware that another guide might make a different selection of buildings and places.

This book can actually be treated as a guided tour from a point of view of time and orientation, and that is why I did not include more places. I suggest one should see the South side on one day and the North side on another. Alternatively, one could leave out every other place in this book and see both North and South sides in one day. Dublin Castle was excluded from this tour as there are excellent guided tours available all week.

With the exception of the James Joyce Museum in Sandycove and the Marino Casino in Clontarf all the places are in geographical order and marked on a map in the back of the book.

I would like to thank the friends in Dublin, in particular Prof. Kevin Nowlan, who have helped and advised me while I was writing this guide.

This was never my town,
I was not born nor bred
Nor schooled here and she will not
Have me alive or dead
But yet she holds my mind
With her seedy elegance,
With her gentle veils of rain
And all her ghosts that walk
And all that hide behind
Her Georgian facades,
The catcalls and the pain,
The glamour of her squalor,
The bravado of her talk.

Louis MacNeice

Introduction

Dublin is beautiful and ugly, cosmopolitan and provincial; it is full of contradictions and therefore eludes an easy description. The muddy waters of the Liffey, which divide it into a North and South side, flow past an extraordinary variety of buildings. They illustrate the history of the town architecturally. Among red brick and crumbling houses of every kind the most striking landmarks on the river are: St Paul's Church with its concrete Grotto, the majestic Four Courts, Christ Church Cathedral, Liberty Hall, and the beautiful Custom House.

Dublin's atmosphere is made up of many things: the beauty of its original layout and architecture, the seediness of its slums, the gentle flow of Liffey and canals and the life of universities and pubs. Above all it lies in the character of its people. Their friendliness and curiosity about other people has made Dublin one of the most welcoming cities to the visitor and one of the easiest cities to live in. No question put to a Dubliner will go unanswered. He has opinions on everything, and likes to express these as often as possible. He loves words, drama, stories, poetry and gossip rather than visual things like pictures, clothes and the appearance of his house.

The large number of young children taking part in Dublin street life is striking. It is not unusual to see them selling newspapers, carrying messages or just loitering about begging for pennies. Perhaps this, more than anything else, gives Dublin the character of a Dickens novel. The horse and cart contributes to the Victorian atmosphere, but this is gradually disappearing under the growing pressure of modern traffic.

Other features remain:

The open markets in Moore Street and Thomas Street where fruit, fish and vegetables are sold with much shouting and gesticulating; Dublin women sitting at street corners selling flowers that are stuffed into prams, in which a dozen children or so were probably reared; Bewley's old fashioned coffee-houses, where one can get the best cup of coffee in Dublin for 1/1; public houses like the Brazen Head, the Mooney pubs or Keogh's in South Anne Street. Some of them like McDaid's in Harry

McDaid's Bar

Street and Mulligan's in Poolbeg Street are meeting places for the Dublin literary set. Members of this are easily recognized in the conventionally unconventional longhaired and bearded youths who hang around the poets or are poets themselves. Some of the old pubs used to be, and a few still are, grocery shops at the same time. Goods like margarine, sugar and baked beans stand beside bottles of liquor on their shelves. Exhausted housewives can drop in, do their shopping and succumb to the temptation of having a quick pint before returning to their old tenements or modern council flats. Recently many old pubs have been expensively converted into soft-carpeted, well-ventilated lounges that have nothing in common with the hazy atmosphere of familiar old pubs. Their 'decor' is rich in bright colours and soft music pursues one even to the lavatories. Apart from the usual drinks colourful cocktails of every kind are prepared behind shiny barcounters. These pubs often have excellent sandwiches and salads. They are frequented at lunch time by Dublin business men—who look like any other business men. There are 851 licensed houses, 221 with off-licenses and 136 clubs; a total of 1,208 places where drink can be obtained. This is an enormous number for a population of some 600,000.

Considering the great popularity of television it is amazing how many theatres are still open. Their success relies mainly on the traditional and established plays of Irish writers like Synge, O'Casey, Brendan Behan and Samuel Beckett. Dubliners have a genuine interest in the theatre and for them the outing is not so much a social occasion. In their casual clothes they make a startling contrast to the dressed-up tourist. The tourist has probably looked forward to the occasion for weeks. His vague impression of Dublin may derive from names like the

Abbey Theatre, Yeats and Oscar Wilde, and the Horse Show in August. Perhaps he had a romantic vision of a fishing town, also the capital of Ireland, out of which world-famous writers like James Joyce and G. B. Shaw mysteriously emerged.

It is quite likely he had no idea that Dublin has some 600,000 inhabitants, and that at least one third of them live in modern suburbs, mostly vast stereotype housing estates with no character at all. In some of these children grow up without a playground or a tree. The most imposing one of them, the Ballymun Housing Estate, consists of gigantic blocks of flats which can be seen on the horizon from many parts of Dublin. Then there are the more residential housing estates. Rows and rows of identical houses with cherry trees and roses in neat front gardens, the only mark of individuality in the choice of curtains

Georgian Doorway

and the colour of the front door. These suburbs can be found everywhere and the visitor will not remember them.

Perhaps the strongest impression Dublin leaves on him is that of eighteenth century brick streets. It not only reminds him of the Georgian era, but it is the Dublin associated with James Joyce, Sean O'Casey and other distinguished writers who made it famous throughout the world. Houses with elegant windows and doors over which elaborate fanlights are often sadly missing, look charming in their very uniformity. In between there are classical eighteenth and nineteenth century stone buildings. In many cases these were designed by distinguished architects from all over Europe, and built by Irish craftsmen whose superb skill has made it possible for us to admire them now. Here and there are yawning gaps where stark office blocks seem to

View of Guinness Brewery

13

spring up overnight, reminding us rather aggressively of the more modern aspects of Dublin.

Since Dublin is the heart of the country from which most roads radiate it has become the centre of its new industries. These consist mainly of assembly industries using raw materials from abroad and plants for the processing of Ireland's agricultural produce for export. A few old industries like the Guinness brewery remain. Founded by Arthur Guinness in 1759, it developed into one of the largest brewing concerns in the world. It dominates the South side of the Liffey like a vast empire, owing part of its success to the Dubliners, for most of whom Guinness stout is still indispensable. On some days of the week a rich smell of heated barley spreads around the brewery, almost reaching the boundaries of the Phoenix Park.

Originally formed as a royal deer park, the Phoenix Park is probably unrivalled in the variety of life it holds within its boundaries. A herd of deer is still roaming through its fields and woods, gazed at by Dubliners and tourists alike. In its 1,752 acres of ground stand the residences of the President of Ireland, the American Ambassador and the Papal Nuncio. It has a racecourse, a polo ground, a cricket, and several hurling pitches. And a zoo which was founded in 1830 and looks more like a private garden with glowing flowerbeds, shrubs, trees, waterfalls and ponds. It is a curious fact that the Dublin Zoo is particularly successful in the breeding of lions. Horse lovers can be seen riding across the soft grassland and picnic enthusiasts seem to prefer sitting on the roadside surrounded by miles of beautiful parkland. The Phoenix Park is an important centre of sport, but by no means the only one. Dublin has three racecourses, two greyhound tracks, about half a dozen Tennis clubs and dozens of well

14

kept golf links. One of them, Portmarnock, is a beautifully situated seaside course and has been mentioned as one of the six finest golf links in the world. An essential part of playing golf in Ireland is the social get-together after the play in the club bar while innumerable rounds of drinks are served.

The biggest sports event of the year is the Dublin Horse Show, competently organized and staged every August by the Royal Dublin Society. The Society was founded in 1731 by fourteen Dublin gentlemen for the 'improvement of husbandry, manufactures and other useful arts and sciences'. Originally called the 'Dublin Society' it was renamed the 'Royal Dublin Society' in 1831. Apart from the Horse Show the Society also stages the Bull Show in March and the Spring Show in May, and it has contributed greatly to cultural activities in Dublin.

For Horse Show Week visitors from all over the world arrive in Dublin and the horsy country population springs to life. There is great excitement and tension in the air, when big show competitions take place. Ireland's best horses are classified and judged by experts, while petal-headed ladies betray rare emotions. There are jumping events, overflowing bars, brassbands playing in the gardens and people scrambling about feeding and grooming well bred horses. In the evening the endless round of cocktail and dinner parties is followed by huge hunt balls in the big Dublin hotels. These are noisily attended by debutantes and their escorts from England. With all the festivities and money-spending during this time most Dubliners profit indirectly from the Horse Show. But few of them are concerned with it and many ignore it. It is really part of the country life which seems to have lost its way into Dublin.

The country is very close. A soft skyline of mountains rises on one side of the town and can be seen

15

from most streets and houses on a clear day. It only takes about half an hour to drive to the top of the Dublin mountains. On weekdays one can still walk for miles without seeing more than a handful of people or a car. Apart from the mountainy horizon, Dublin's skyline shows a dense forest of TV aerials. They have to be bigger than aerials in England as most Dubliners like to watch BBC and Ulster Television as well as the home station, Radio Telefís Eireann.

The enormous number of domes and spires is another striking feature of Dublin. The two big cathedrals are Protestant, although over eighty per cent of the population are Catholics, and the Catholic Cathedral stands in a narrow side street. An astonishing number of pretty churches belong to the Church of Ireland (the Protestant church) built in its heyday in the eighteenth century. Many of their congregations have dwindled to such an extent that they have had to be closed. Whereas even on a weekday there·is a steady trickle of people coming out of and going into the neo-classical Catholic churches, built in the nineteenth century after Catholic Emancipation was achieved by Daniel O'Connell. Dublin has brought forward many great men whose statues are sprinkled all over the town and make us aware of its unusually intricate history.

Dublin is not representative of the whole country but it is the centre of Ireland and one of the best loved capitals in the world.

A Sketch of Dublin's History

Keystone on Custom House

Dublin was never a Gaelic city although we read Gaelic names on street signs and can look at a unique collection of early Irish art in the National Museum and the famous book of Kells in Trinity College. The Norse founded *Dyfflin* in the ninth century. Attracted by its geographical position on the mouth of a river, with a large bay stretching towards the sea, and sheltered by mountains on one side, they conveniently conducted their plundering raids on monastic settlements from here. It was not till 1014 that the Irish, under Brian Boru, defeated them and confined their conquering pursuits to the coastline. But the Norse, gradually integrating with the Irish, stayed in possession of Dublin till the arrival of the Normans. Now only a few names such as Skerries, Leixlip, Oxmantown and Howth remind us of the Scandinavians in Dublin.

In 1169 Anglo-Norman adventurers came to Ireland. After their seizure of Dublin under Strongbow, Henry II, who feared their independence in Ireland, granted the city to the citizens of Bristol with the free custom and liberties of their native city. In the winters of 1171 and 1172 he held court in

17

Dublin, laid the basis of an English administration and received submission from several Irish chieftains and princes. From this time Dublin was controlled by the English until Ireland became independent in 1922. For long their power did not extend much beyond the Pale, that area around Dublin protected by a ring of castles. By the beginning of the sixteenth century the Pale stretched over about sixty miles in length and thirty miles in width.

Dublin Castle was erected in King John's times on the site of an old Norse fortress. It became the seat of the Viceroys, who were the representatives of the English Crown. Early medieval Dublin was about half a mile long and one quarter of a mile wide, surrounded by a thick wall, which was fortified by towers. The Liffey bordered it on the North side, the little river Poddle—later led underground—on the South side. With the exception of parts of old towers in Dublin Castle only ecclesiastical buildings and fragments of the medieval wall remain of Anglo-Norman Dublin. Of the still existing building Christ Church Cathedral and St Audoens lay within its walls, St Patricks and on the North side of the Liffey St Michans and the Cistercian Abbey of St Marys lay without. The vast task of building the quays and the North and South walls was not undertaken until the eighteenth century. The river was much wider, the sea much nearer and most land east of where O'Connell bridge is now, unreclaimed swamp land. Dublin's citizens in the middle ages must have been constantly aware of the sea—both as a natural danger and as an ever-present reminder of the threat of invasion.

They lived in timber and wattle dwellings, most of them single story cabins. Excavations which are being carried out in High Street, have disclosed that street levels have risen fourteen feet through continual build-up since the ninth century. Unfortunately cellar-buildings in the Georgian period claimed eight feet of this build-up which in many layers contains fascinating relics of medieval Dublin life, and is now precious ground for archaeologists. Finds are particularly interesting because they not only include completed articles, but pieces in various unfinished stages of manufacture. Many of them point to the skilful use of metal, leather and bone; examples can be admired in the National Museum in Kildare Street. Work and craftsmanship gave a new status to the citizens of medieval Dublin of which it has been said: 'Freedom, corporate equality, democratic participation, autonomy, were never fully achieved in any medieval town; but there was perhaps a greater measure of these qualities there than had been exhibited before, even in Greece. For a brief while "communitas" triumphed over "dominium".'

Apart from the flourishing development of crafts and the forming of Trade Guilds which eventually grew into the municipal government, Dublin changed very little during the middle ages. It continued to be the scene of strife between unyielding deputies and Irish rebels. A large number of these rebels were Anglo-Normans who had become 'more Irish than the Irish' and had failed in their allegiance to the crown. Eventually, as English power grew throughout Ireland, most of the rebels were deprived of their land and supplanted by English settlers.

Dublin was to witness historical events of both splendour and violence. In 1484 Lambert Simnel, a Yorkist was crowned king of England in Christ Church Cathedral. An army in support of this boy pretender subsequently invaded England, but was defeated. Another turbulent event was the fatal

19

revolt of Silken Thomas Fitzgerald, eldest son of the ninth Earl of Kildare, in 1534. He mistakenly believed that his father, who had been summoned to England and had entrusted him with the government during his absence, had been executed in London. With an army he rode into Dublin to St Marys, flung his sword of State—symbol of the Viceroys—on the table and declared open rebellion. This cost him and his five Geraldine uncles their lives and almost extinguished the greatest Anglo-Irish family of that time.

With Henry VIII, who made himself 'the Supreme Head On Earth of the whole Church of Ireland', the Reformation came to Ireland. It was associated with English rule and in many parts of the country, including Ulster, the Anglicization of Ireland was stubbornly opposed and a series of bitter wars ensued. In 1649 Oliver Cromwell landed in Dublin with a Puritan army and proceeded to subdue the Catholics. He desecrated their churches and transferred their sources of wealth to Protestants. By the end of the Cromwellian period Dublin had deteriorated badly. St Patricks and Christ Church Cathedral and most of its buildings were more or less ruined. The wall with its towers and gates decaying fast and the castle was described as 'the worst castle in the worst situation in Christendom'. Even the population had shrunk to 9,000 souls.

Over the next 140 years Dublin was to change from a shabby medieval town into a metropolis of such size and beauty that in both respects it was the second city of the British empire. This was largely due to the Duke of Ormond, one of the most popular and circumspect viceroys, who returned from his exile in France in 1662. It has been said that with him the Renaissance came to Ireland. Perhaps influenced by his recent visit to the continent, the

Duke of Ormond believed in centralizing power in the country.

Ormond intended to build a ceremonial capital of which the Irish could be proud. From now on Dublin established itself as the political centre of Ireland, permanently holding the seat of Parliament. It was also the main sea port and trading centre of Ireland and there was a steady flow of adventurers and settlers of every kind from abroad. In 1682 the surveyor and economist Sir William Petty estimated the population to be 58,000. After the famous battle of the Boyne in 1690, in which William of Orange defeated the Catholic King James II, and the subsequent cruel enforcement of the 'Penal Laws', which deprived Catholics of all rights, the Protestant Ascendancy Class at last felt secure.

It is an astonishing thought that at this time, one hundred years after the foundation of Trinity College, wheat was still growing less than half a mile from the college. The rapid growth of the city brought along acute social problems. The squalid living conditions of the working classes drove Jonathan Swift, Dean of St Patricks and one of the most dynamic and effective men Dublin ever saw, to write his 'Modest Proposal'. In this acid satire Swift suggested the killing of little children to provide 'a most delicious, nourishing and wholesome food'. Paradoxically the great era of building and expansion in this very field began, while Swift was writing furious pamphlets. He was surrounded and loved by the poor of Dublin, many of whom lived in the Liberties near St Patricks Cathedral. Irish peers and Members of Parliament built themselves fine stone mansions and the city, side by side with private speculators, carried out grand improvement schemes. In the Georgian Society Records of 1911 J. P. Mahaffy wrote: 'There is no doubt whatever that almost all the fine houses in old Dublin were built by and for the landed gentry, and from their profits as the owners of estates let to tenants.'

In 1707 the Ballast Office started building the North and South walls along the Liffey and stone quays were gradually opened up. As the traffic between the South and North side grew in the middle of the eighteenth century new bridges were laid across the Liffey. In 1757 the city set up the 'Commissioners for Making Wide and Convenient Streets', in 1763 the 'Commissioners for Making the Circular Roads', in 1773 the 'Paving Board' for paving, cleaning, lighting, draining and improving the streets. In the 1790s the two canals, the Grand and the Royal, running parallel to the circular roads, were completed. When Malton was finishing his drawings of Dublin buildings in 1799, Dublin was about seven miles in circumference and the number of inhabitants was estimated at 200,000.

The first of Dublin's famous private developers was the banker Luke Gardiner. He laid out Henrietta Street in the 1720s and later Sackville Street—now O'Connell Street—and Rutland Square—now Parnell Square. Mountjoy Square followed at the end of the eighteenth century. His great rival who was to surpass him ultimately was Lord Fitzwilliam. He developed the area around Leinster House, including Fitzwilliam Square and Merrion Square in the second half of the eighteenth century. The North-East side was the fashionable quarter during the first half of the eighteenth century, but after the Earl of Kildare built his town house on the South side, fashion moved South too. Gardiner carried on the developments on the North side successfully until he was killed in 1798. The trade and craftsmen, notably the weaving community, settled in the South-West of Dublin around

Cork Street and the Coombe. The North West remained fairly empty and later became a building ground for jails, hospitals and lunatic asylums. They were advanced and far sighted by any standards in Europe.

Apart from these big schemes, imposing public buildings went up, as if to consolidate and hold Dublin's power. Of many distinguished buildings Sir Edward Lovett Pearce's Parliament House, now the Bank of Ireland, and later James Gandon's Four Courts and Custom House may be the most important ones of the eighteenth century. There was a great revival in the arts and although the cattle and woollen trades had been at first crippled by English restrictions, other industries, notably the linen industries, were flourishing. Dublin Society entertained lavishly and extravagantly and, as the eighteenth century progressed, became more liberal in its thinking. Gradually the penal laws were relaxed, but it was 130 years before the last of them was repealed. The last quarter of the eighteenth century, particularly, saw a happy expansion in every field which could not be halted abruptly even by political disasters.

The Act of Union of 1800, imposed by Britain in an orgy of corruption, abolished the Irish Parliament which had become semi-independent in 1782 under Henry Grattan's leadership. It subjected Ireland directly to the Parliament at Westminster. The abortive revolution of the United Irishmen in 1798 hastened the moves to unite the two kingdoms. Under leaders like Wolfe Tone, they had tried to set up an independent Irish republic. Tone was captured in a French ship off Lough Swilly, when he tried to bring over the French to assist the Irish cause. Later he committed suicide in prison.

As travelling grew less hazardous, more and more

23

visitors came to Dublin. On the whole they were astonished and surprised by its beauty and scale and most of them compared it to London.

In 1810 one of them wrote:

'There is something inexpressibly graceful in the appearance of this town to a stranger; he is forcibly struck with the strong likeness it bears to London, of which it is a beautiful copy . . .; the streets are wide and commodious, the houses uniform, lofty and elegant.'

Others were struck by the extreme poverty of the working classes and the enormous number of beggars. In 1824 an American citizen who published a book entitled *Sketches of Rambles in North Britain and Ireland,* described Dublin thus:

'Nothing short of actual vision can convey to an American a just conception of the apparent misery of this class of people in Ireland. In Dublin mendicants swarm the streets in every direction, and assail the passenger with an importunity which cannot, or will not, be repulsed. In the more frequented quarter of the city, one of these wretched objects is seen lying upon the door-steps of almost every respectable dwelling. Families are literally strewn along the principal street, at intervals of a few yards, clothed with fragments of garments which gave me the first distinct notion of tatters . . . Mendicity in my opinion has reached its "ne plus ultra" in this city.'

J. P. Mahaffy brilliantly described society in Georgian Dublin in a long essay in the Third Volume of the Georgian Records. He was neither blinded by the aesthetic splendour of its life nor did he fail to record all aspects of its highly developed culture because of its inherent vices.

24

After Robert Emmet's rising in 1803 which led to his capture and execution a long period of political stagnation followed. In 1829 Catholic Emancipation, giving Catholics the right to sit in Parliament, was passed by the Parliament at Westminster. Daniel O'Connell who later became Lord Mayor of Dublin had led the Catholic Association during its struggle for freedom. He also formed the Repeal Association to repeal the Act of Union. This failed in the end, but out of it sprang the 'Young Ireland' movement which was to influence later generations of Irish people to a great extent. Although their rising in 1848 was unsuccessful, it was an indication of national feeling in Ireland.

In the years 1845–49 the great famine, caused by the potatoe blight, swept Ireland. Dublin became a huge camp for starving refugees from the country and the government set up soup kitchens to relieve starvation. While the Irish population shrank from eight and a half to six and a half million in these years, partly due to death and partly emigration, Dublin's population increased to over 300,000. The city expanded rapidly beyond the canals, and circular roads and suburbs spread into the countryside. With the growing strength of the Catholic middle classes Catholic churches were going up everywhere and the Catholic University was founded in 1854. In 1872 horse trams were first seen in Dublin and by this time all the great stations had been built. Perhaps they were the most notable contribution of the nineteenth century to Dublin architecture. The first railway line had been opened up in 1834, when Dublin was linked with Kingstown—now Dun Laoghaire.

In the 1890s Irish people felt disillusioned after the fall of Charles Stewart Parnell. He had led the Home Rule Party with great success until his affair with Kitty O'Shea was revealed in a divorce case. After Parnell's fall and death in 1891, the Home Rule Movement lost its strength and a decade of political strife and ineffectiveness set in.

Slums developed as better-off people moved to the suburbs; the North side particularly fell into decay. Although the relative decline of Dublin after the Union made the redundance and deterioration of some parts of Dublin inevitable, it was unfortunate that the North side should have been affected so severely. While the South side was flat and allowed Fitzwilliam's classical and correct planning, the slightly hilly North side with Luke Gardiner's imaginative street designs must at that time have been even more beautiful.

When, at the end of this century, the Gaelic League was founded by Dr Douglas Hyde and Eoin MacNeill, Dublin began to be the centre of the national cultural revival. The aim of the league was to keep and restore the Irish language and make Irish people conscious of their own ancient culture. It quickly gained popular appeal and became a nationalist political pressure group. Beside it grew the Irish Literary Revival, led by William Butler Yeats. With Lady Gregory, George Russell, J. M. Synge, George Moore, James Stephens and others Yeats revived interest in old Irish folklore and sagas. They created the Irish Literary Theatre which produced plays that were to become world famous; most of them are still performed by the Abbey Theatre.

Years of agitation by the Sinn Feiners, the Gaelic League, the I.R.B. and other patriot movements culminated in the Rising of 1916. The Irish revolutionaries, led by Padraig Pearse and James Connolly seized the General Post Office in O'Connell Street and issued a proclamation of the Provisional

Government of the Irish Republic. After a week of fighting during which Lower O'Connell Street was burnt down, the rebellion was suppressed and the fifteen leaders were executed. These executions played into the hands of the revolutionary movement, making martyrs of the executed leaders. A wave of sympathy and identification with the revolutionary cause swept the country. The War of Independence, better known as The Troubles, broke out in 1919. This finally led to the Anglo-Irish Treaty of 1922, making twenty-six counties of Ireland a Free State, though the North, predominantly loyal to the Crown, was partitioned and the six north-eastern counties left in the United Kingdom. After yet another war, this time a civil war between supporters and opposers of the terms of the Treaty with the United Kingdom, Ireland at last found independence. Dublin then became the capital of a separate nation with its own Parliament.

Tour of the South Side of Dublin

Leinster House—seat of the Irish Parliament

In 1744, on the death of his father, James Fitzgerald became the twentieth Earl of Kildare and inherited a considerable fortune. Only twenty-two years of age, he had already travelled the continent and sat in Parliament for the borough of Athy. Finding the Fitzgerald townhouse in Suffolk Street inadequate, he employed Richard Castle to build a new town residence for him. Richard Castle demanded a large open space to give his imagination and architectural talent full scope, which accounts for the rural character of the house. Land was purchased in Molesworth fields and the building of Kildare House, as it was first called, began in 1745. At that time the North side was fashionable and land lying East of Coote Lane—renamed Kildare Street in 1745—was open country stretching towards the Wicklow Hills. When society in Dublin showed surprise about Kildare's bold move to the South East he announced: 'They will follow, wherever I go.' This statement was proved right within a few years.

The building of Kildare House took two years. Meanwhile the Earl had married the beautiful Lady Emily Lennox who could hardly wait for 'her charming great house' to be finished. In 1766 the Earl of Kildare was created Duke of Leinster which gave the house its name. Chiefly interested and involved in politics, he also carried out grand improvements on his country estate Carton in Kildare. His wife Emily who married again after his death in 1773 had seventeen children. One of them was Lord Edward Fitzgerald, of whom Sir John Doyle said: 'I never knew so lovable a person.' Lord Edward wrote to his mother in 1794: 'I confess Leinster House does not inspire the brightest ideas. By-the-by, what a melancholy house it is.'

The second Duke of Leinster, William Robert, was extremely popular and of a kind nature. As Colonel of the first Dublin Regiment of the Irish Volunteers, he held many reviews on Leinster Lawn. He opposed the Union and died at Carton in 1804. In 1815 the third Duke of Leinster sold the mansion to the Dublin Society for £10,000 and a perpetual rent of £900 per annum. The Dublin Society occupied it from 1820 to 1921, adding a number of buildings on either side in the second half of the nineteenth century. These included museums, the National Gallery, the National Library and School of Art. In 1921 the Irish Free State chose Leinster House as the meeting place for the Oireachtas, the Irish Parliament. Seanad Eireann, the Senate, sits in the magnificent saloon, decorated with plasterwork in the Adam style, in the North wing. Dail Eireann, the House of Representatives, occupies the remodelled lecture theatre on the South side, which was originally added by the Royal Dublin Society.

The stark building is of hard Ardbraccan stone, quarried in County Meath. It has two stories and is built like a classical Irish country house in the shape of a rectangle with a central corridor on the main axis. The magnificent entrance-hall has a coved ceiling and leads on to fine rooms which were redecorated towards the end of the eighteenth century. James Wyatt carried out most of the work.

It is asserted that the basic design of the White House is a copy of Leinster House. James Hoban, born in Carlow in 1762, who had studied at the architectural school of the Dublin Society, was the architect who won the White House Competition in 1792. In 1794 Thomas Malton described Leinster House as 'the most stately private edifice in the city ... enjoying in the tumult of a noisy metropolis all the retirement of the country'.

Opening Times

The public is admitted to the debates of both Houses. Admission tickets may be obtained from deputies or senators or from the Superintendent. The principal rooms are open to visitors when the House is not in session. From Mondays to Fridays (incl.) 10 a.m.–12.30 p.m., 2 p.m.–4.30 p.m. Closed on Saturdays and Sundays.

Merrion Square

Merrion Square, view of Mount St and St Stephen's Church

One of the most beautiful features of Dublin are the great Georgian squares. The contrast between restrained uniform brick houses and rich green parks is subtle. It gives Dublin a dignity which it is in danger of losing through its modern town planning. Merrion Square may owe its good state of preservation not only to its comparatively young age—St Stephen's Green was laid out almost a hundred years earlier—but also to Leinster House.

Recognizing the coming trend of the nobility to move near Leinster House, the sixth Lord Fitzwilliam began to develop Meryon's land in the middle of the eighteenth century. The Fitzwilliams and the Gardiners became the famous landlords of Dublin. In fact they, like Trinity College, were tenants of the city themselves.

Starting on the North side in 1762 John Ensor laid out a large handsome square which was not completed till the end of the century. In 1787, by which time houses had gone up on the South and East, an observer wrote that most of the houses on the North side were of granite stone as far as the first floor 'which gives them an air of magnificence inferior to nothing of the kind if we except Bath'. Most houses were built of red- or maroon-coloured brick. They often went up in pairs or in groups of three, always conforming to the general lay-out, but never matching the neighbouring houses completely. The restraint of these houses only enhances the beautiful doors with their graceful fanlights. The latter ones became wider and wider as the square grew, carried by columns or pilasters. Originally these were said to have been put in as a protection against thieves. The balconies—more often cast than wrought iron —were added later.

Merrion Square became more and more fashionable towards the end of the eighteenth century. In

1794 the following description of the festivities at Antrim House appeared in the *Anthologia Hibernica*:

'This day se'nnight the Marchioness of Antrim gave a most superb rout, ball and supper, at her ladyship's house in Merrion Square, to a most brilliant and extremely numerous assemblage of the first rank and fashions. His Excellency the Lord Lieutenant and most of the nobility of the town were present. . . . Dancing commenced at 11 o'clock, and at 1 the company were summoned to the supper rooms, where elegance and plenty seemed to vie in the decoration of the festive board—while wit, beauty and all the gaiety and splendour of fashion enlivened the enchanting scene. Dancing was resumed after supper, and the company separated with reluctance at 6 o'clock in the morning.'

J. P. Mahaffy wrote that in the first half of the century 'the separation between residential streets for the gentry and slums for the poor had not yet become marked. Evidences of squalor were to be seen in all the leading thoroughfares, in which beggars were even more frequent than they are now, and into which pigs and cattle made dangerous irruption.'

In 1769 Arthur Wellesley, later Duke of Wellington, was born in Mornington House, No 24 Merrion Street. His father, the Earl of Mornington, was Professor of Music in Trinity College. He gave many popular concerts with an orchestra which was led by him and 'manned by noblemen and gentlemen'. In 1848 the second Lord Cloncurry wrote that his father had bought Mornington House in 1791 for £8,000 and that it was sold shortly after the Union for £2,500. It now houses the Land Commission.

After the Union the houses of those peers and parliamentarians who left Dublin were taken up by judges and others from the legal profession, eventually replaced by the medical profession. Now Merrion Square holds embassies, offices of every kind, and headquarters of various cultural and scientific institutions. The building standing on the South side of Leinster Lawn houses the Natural History Division of the National Museum, and was erected by Sir Thomas Deane II. The extensions of Sir Charles Lanyon's National Gallery (1859–60) were also by Deane. The National Gallery was built with subscriptions in memory of William Dargan. He was a rich and public-spirited railway entrepreneur, well known for organizing the Industrial Exhibition on Leinster Lawn in 1853. Among several monuments decorating the lawn there is one of him by Thomas Farrell, R.H.A., and one of George Bernard Shaw by Troubetsky. Shaw left the gallery a third of his estate. He once wrote that he owed his education more to the days spent at the Gallery than to those spent at school. It owns a superb collection of Italian paintings, even a Michelangelo, and is rich in the Dutch, Spanish and English schools which include Rubens, Goya and ten major works by Gainsborough. The fine Irish collection includes John Butler Yeats, Hone, Osborne, Lavery, Orpen, as well as good examples of early Irish painting. The Director of the National Gallery is James White.

The Rutland Memorial, a beautiful little fountain with coade stone ornaments stands opposite the National Gallery. It was designed by Henry Aaron Baker, a pupil of James Gandon's, in 1791.

Famous people who once lived in the square, include Daniel O'Connell (1775–1847) in No 58, Sir William and Lady Wilde and their son Oscar in No

Rutland Memorial

1, Joseph Sheridan Le Fanu (1814–73) in No 70, and William Butler Yeats (1865–1939) in No 83.

While there is a brave struggle going for the preservation of Mountjoy Square and St Stephen's Green one can only hope that the beauty of Merrion Square and Fitzwilliam Square with their long, unbroken vistas will remain unmarred.

Opening Times of the National Gallery
Mondays–Saturdays (incl.), from 10 a.m.–6 p.m.; Thursdays, 10 a.m.–9 p.m.; Sundays, 2 p.m.–5 p.m. No charge, catalogues available, also photographs of any item in the collections. During July, August and September there are guided tours on Saturdays, starting at 11 o'clock.

Newman House, Nos 85, 86 St Stephen's Green

Plasterwork in Newman House

St Stephen's Green is the oldest Square in Dublin; the corporation started leasing plots around the old common as early as 1663. It was therefore doomed to deteriorate earlier than the other squares and yield to the pressures of redevelopment. As a result the architecture is extremely varied. Of a few significant landmarks Newman House, incorporating Nos 85 and 86, is the most distinguished. The handsome stone-faced façades of both houses have never been changed since they were built.

The plot of No 85—later called Clanwilliam House—was leased by a Hugh Montgomery in 1738, the house built by Richard Castle in 1740. The Italian stuccadores Paul and Philip Francini decorated it with exceptionally fine plasterwork. The walls of the study, also called the Apollo room, are adorned with the nine muses in plaster panels. The room is dominated by Apollo who stands over the mantelpiece in a gay rococo panel which flows over the ceiling cornice. The theme of classical figures as well as the treatment of it is similar to the Francini work in Riverstown, Glanmire, County Cork (open to the public). The ceiling of the saloon upstairs, which covers the whole length of the house, is a smaller version of the Francini ceiling in Carton, Maynooth (see page 119). It is rich in allegorical figures 'an allegory shall we say of good government and prudent economy exercised over earth, air and water'.

The Francini brothers are responsible for many interiors in Ireland, such as Castletown in County Kildare (see page 116), Carton, Maynooth (see page 119), Riverstown, Glanmire, County Cork, and Kilshannig, County Tipperary. In his book *Dublin Decorative Plasterwork* C. P. Curran wrote about them:

> 'Whatever their origin they represent one of the successive waves of stuccadores who from quite an early period swarmed over Europe from fertile hives in the valleys on either side of the Swiss-Italian Alps. Their history is similar in all countries. The Italians, here as in France and England, practised the human figure in the full scale and realized all its plastic possibilities. At its ordinary level the work of the Francinis is classical and uninspired. At its highest as in the Carton ceiling or the saloon in No 85 St Stephen's Green, it shows the constructive power and the nobility in conception and design which mark the Italian character in Art.'

No 85 changed its occupants frequently. In the

middle of the eighteenth century Richard Chapell Whaley, M.P. for Wicklow, lived in it; Lord and Lady Clanwilliam in the last quarter of the century. 'Burn-Chapel' Whaley is reputed to have been a fierce character who persecuted priests. Yielding to his ambition to own a bigger and more pretentious house than No 85 he built No 86.

In his *Views of Dublin* Malton described No 86 as

'the structure which claims principal attention amongst the edifices in St Stephen's Green ... The House was probably commenced in 1765, for on a stone over the fireplace in the kitchen is carved "16 April 1765 R.C.W.".'

The palatial five bay house with its charming lead lion by John Van Nost, Jr, guarding the porch, abounds in the most imaginative plasterwork. The hand of Robert West, leading Irish exponent of rococo plasterwork and master builder, can clearly be recognized in the motifs. Birds flying and feeding their young, clusters of grapes, fruit, foliage and musical instruments. As in other Irish houses the plasterwork in the staircase hall is bolder and stronger than in the rooms. Unlike in No 85 the human figure does not appear in any form. 'Had No 86 included such figure work in equal excellence to the rest of the decoration, its stucco would stand unrivalled in Dublin.' No 86 was the last of the pre-Adam houses. Richard Chapell Whaley died in 1769, and it is believed that his notorious son Buck, who had become a member of Parliament at eighteen, lived in No 86 for some time. He was one of the most eccentric of all Dublin rakes and was well known in gambling circles. One night at a dinner party in Leinster House he bet £15,000 that he would walk to Jerusalem. He duly achieved this in 1789 after a year's journey which cost him £8,000.

He wrote of this journey that it was: 'the only instance in all my life before, in which any of my projects turned out to my advantage'.

In 1853 Clanwilliam House and No 86 were bought by Cardinal Cullen to form the centre of the Catholic University of Ireland. It opened in 1854 and John Henry Newman was its first rector. In 1909 the Jesuit University College, where James Joyce, Patrick H. Pearse and Eamonn de Valera had been students, was succeeded by a college of the new National University of Ireland.

University College Dublin

Until 1851 Trinity College stood alone in Ireland as a seat of advanced education. It was founded in Queen Elizabeth I's reign as a purely Protestant Ascendancy establishment.

In 1851 a new Catholic University was set up with Colleges at Dublin, Belfast, Cork and Galway. These were originally known as the 'Queen's Colleges' as Belfast still is. After 1920 the Belfast College was divorced from the others which are now known as the National University of Ireland. Dublin is naturally the most important of the three, and has far more distinctive native Irish flavour than Trinity. At the same time it has an international reputation and is attended by many foreigners.

Its original headquarters was at 85 and 86 St Stephen's Green and over the years it has acquired property all over the Dublin area. One of its latest and greatest acquisitions is the Lyons estate near Celbridge where it has 1,300 acres for the Faculty of Agriculture.

Now Newman House holds the club and recreational rooms of University College. It is one of the few important Dublin houses that is in safe and appreciative hands.

Opening Times

Application for admission should be made to the College authorities.

Powerscourt House

For most people Powerscourt House stands for Powerscourt, Enniskerry, County Wicklow (see page 125). Since they are not aware of the Powerscourt House in Dublin—once the town house of the Viscounts Powerscourt—they must be amazed when they catch sight of it as they walk along South William Street. This gigantic building would be outstanding in any great square or plaza in Europe. Indeed it would be an advantage to see it from a distance. Standing in a charming, but very narrow back street which runs parallel to Grafton Street, one cannot take in the royal scale of this palace. Once again, the luxury and splendour in which the aristocracy lived in Dublin during the eighteenth century astonishes us.

The palladian front rises majestically above neighbouring houses with an attic that is said to have been built for an observatory. The house is built of dark granite, quarried on the Powerscourt estate in Wicklow. The coarse texture of the façade gives no hint of the delicate decoration inside.

The third Viscount Powerscourt commissioned the Irish architect Robert Mack to build him a town house. No other important building is attributed to Mack. Powerscourt House was begun in 1771 and finished in 1774. The quantity and quality of the detail distinguishes this house.

It has a fine staircase made of mahogany like the beautifully carved balusters, dado and doors. The ornamented window casings and shutters in the drawing rooms upstairs are unique in Dublin. The plasterwork was done by James McCullagh—master of the Bricklayer's Guild—who decorated the hall and staircase hall—and by Michael Stapleton—the Irish Adam—who is responsible for the drawing rooms upstairs and the dining room downstairs. McCullagh's work is still in the rococo style, although at this late stage it looks subdued and has no trace of Robert West's creative design.

Michael Stapleton's work was done only a few years later, yet the contrast is stunning. The relief is low, the strictest symmetry reigns, the lacelike patterns look delightful on the walls and ceilings. These were cast from moulds that could be used again and again; the art of handmoulded plaster-work had come to an end. The dining room walls are decorated with medallions of popular and repetitive themes, held by delicate garlands of

42

Plasterwork in Powerscourt House

plasterwork. These medallions came into fashion for a short time. For some time Stapleton resided at No 1 Mountjoy Square, where he decorated several houses. He was the master of plaster decoration in the silver age, the period when plaster decoration last flourished as an art.

In 1807 the fourth Viscount Powerscourt sold the house for £15,000 to the Commissioners of Stamp Duty, who added buildings in the pretty courtyard behind the house. In 1832 the present owners Ferrier, Pollock & Co. Ltd., wholesale drapers, purchased the house. It is in good repair and every room is used either for office purposes or as a storeroom.

Opening Times
Due to the understanding and kindness of the directors of Ferrier, Pollock & Co. Ltd., visitors can see the house inside during normal office hours.

Mondays–Fridays (incl.) 9 a.m.–1.15 p.m., 2.30 p.m.–5.30 p.m. Closed on Saturdays.

Trinity College

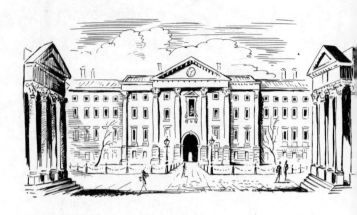

A few landmarks on Dublin's earliest map—John Speed 1610—include Queen Elizabeth I's 'College of the Holy and Undivided Trinity', which was founded in 1592 to educate the sons of the Anglo-Irish Ascendancy class. Its foundation was part of the Reformation in Ireland. Always Protestant in character and tradition Trinity College has been liberal in its policies from a very early age. It first admitted Roman Catholics in 1793, although it was not till 1873 that they could acquire fellowships and scholarships. Like Oxford and Cambridge it has a distinctly English, yet international atmosphere, with students from all over the globe mingling with Irish and English students. Walking from College Green through an archway into the cobblestoned Parliament Square one has a feeling of walking into England's last stronghold in Ireland. And yet members of this University have often been closely linked with the Irish side in politics; it brought forward many of Ireland's greatest patriots.

No buildings of its early days remain. The Rubrics on the East side of the old library is said to date from before 1700, but in his book *Dublin 1680–1880* Maurice Craig doubts this. The college must have suffered considerably during the Cromwellian and later Jacobite Wars in the seventeenth century.

On his arrival in Ireland in 1689 James II seized Trinity to use it as a barracks and appointed the only Catholic Provost in its history, the Rev Michael Moore. The latter preserved a whole epoch of culture in Ireland by saving the library with its priceless early manuscripts from Jacobite troops. The library, erected between 1712 and 1732 by the Surveyor General of Ireland, Colonel Thomas Burgh, is now the oldest building in Trinity. Originally it had an open loggia to prevent dampness creeping in. Unfortunately this was filled in to make further room for books. Trinity Library is one of the copyright libraries, entitled to a free copy of every work published in Great Britain and Ireland. It holds over a million printed volumes and Ireland's greatest collection of MSS and historical documents; its catalogue dates from 1603.

The entrance hall of the library has a staircase hall by Richard Castle (1750) and rococo plaster by Edward Semple. In 1857 Benjamin Woodward changed the library by making the Long Room on the first floor and the one below into one, crowning it with a timber barrel vault. (A more detailed description of the contents of the library, some of which is on display, follows at the end of this chapter.)

The next building to go up was the old Printing House, given to the college by John Stearne, Bishop of Clogher. Richard Castle finished it in 1734. It stands on the North West side of the Rubrics and looks like a Doric temple.

Between 1745 and 1749 the Dining Hall was built on the North East side of the Chapel, also to the design of Castle. Shortly afterwards it was rebuilt, most likely to the same design. At this time Richard Baldwin ruled over the college with an iron hand, trying to restore discipline which had gradually disappeared during the troubled times. With a dynamic personality he tried to keep both students and Fellows in order, a great task at a time when violence was still rampant in Dublin. The college boys took great delight in participating in the street battles.

In 1734 one of the Fellows was murdered in Trinity College by rebelling students. Some of these were expelled and prosecuted by the College, but to no avail. Maurice Craig wrote about this with an ironic touch:

'Good society in Dublin (which was Tory) was scandalized at "so cruel a persecution against the sons of gentlemen", who were "suspected only of a frolick," and was most incensed against these Whig dons, who, being, after all, only a sort of glorified schoolmasters, were middle-class at the best.'

Baldwin died in 1758 and was succeeded by Francis Andrews, a man of great charm and social talents, which were to benefit the college to a great extent. As Member for Derry he was an excellent speaker in Parliament, which gave Trinity handsome grants. It paid for the erection of the new West front which had been begun in 1752, and was finished in 1759 by Keane and Sanderson, London. The great Corinthian front of Trinity faces the old Parliament House where many of its students became famous members. On weekdays this classical façade is enlivened by tourists and university members

46

swarming in and out of the archway in the centre.

After completing the West side of Parliament Square Provost Andrews spared no time to accomodate himself in style. In 1759 the Provost's House was built by John Smyth, an Irish architect, under Andrew's close supervision. The design was an adaptation of Burlington's House for General Wade in London. Its façade of blackened sandstone, which was imported from Liverpool, stands South of Trinity's West front and can be admired from the road. It is the only great town mansion in Dublin still privately lived in and used for its original purpose.

Under Hely-Hutchinson's provostship Parliament Square was completed with two magnificent identical buildings facing each other. On the South side stands the Theatre of 1781, now the Examination Hall, by Sir William Chambers with Stapleton plasterwork. It contains fine pictures of several provosts, a superb monument to Baldwin by Christopher Hewetson of Kilkenny, a gilt oak chandelier which used to hang in the House of Commons and an organ case said to have been captured from the Spaniards in 1702. On the North side stands the identical building, the College Chapel, also to Chamber's design. The work was carried out by Graham Meyers between 1779 and 1790, and it was decorated with plasterwork by Michael Stapleton. It has fine wood panelling and nineteenth century stained glass which gives it a gloomy atmosphere.

Sir Jonah Barrington who gave a vivid, if not always accurate picture of Dublin in his *Personal Sketches,* described his time in Trinity thus:

'The college course, at that time, though a very learned one, was ill arranged, pedantic, and

47

totally out of sequence. Students were examined in Locke *On the Human Understanding,* before their own had arrived at the first stage of maturity. We were set to work at the most obstruse sciences before we had well digested the simpler ones. . . .'

There are, however, greater men to remember who studied at Trinity at that time. Theobald Wolfe Tone in particular. Quite a number of students and some Fellows were to join his movement of The United Irishmen. When this leaked out, the Vice-Chancellor, Lord Clare, visited the college himself and made a thorough investigation. Every student was questioned and afterwards nineteen students, among them Robert Emmet, were expelled. Henry Grattan went to Trinity twenty years before Tone. Of many distinguished men who were educated there Jonathan Swift (1667–1745), George Berkeley (1685–1753), Oliver Goldsmith (1728–74) and Edmund Burke (1729–97) were to become world famous. But, according to Sir Walter Scott, Swift 'read and studied' at college more for 'amusement' and to 'divert melancholy reflections' than with the 'zeal of acquiring knowledge'.

The most significant Victorian building is the Museum Building erected between 1853 and 1857 by Thomas Deane and Benjamin Woodward. It is decorated on the outside with fine carvings by the O'Shea brothers. Ruskin admired it so much that he gave Woodward the commission for the Oxford Museum. Now the Engineering and Geological Schools are housed in the Museum Building. At the time of its building Oscar Wilde was born in Dublin; he, too, became a student at Trinity.

Between the Museum building and the old Library another library was erected between 1964 and 1967. This new library is the result of an international competition which created considerable interest attracting over 300 competitors. It is also the result of an unending need for book space required by the college, as well as an urgent need for reader space. The winning design was the work of the architects Ahrends, Burton and Koralek who have since been commissioned to build Trinity's new Arts Building and the G.P.O. headquarters in London.

Built of reinforced white concrete, the library is uncompromisingly different from existing buildings in Trinity. The external wall enclosing the upper floors has an outer leaf of Wicklow granite ashlar blocks. The unadorned walls are set against the flowing curves of the plate glass windows which soften the total impression. It is at the same time a strong and monumental building which manages to be approachable. As one gets to know its interior, one realizes that the almost sculpted forms are not arbitrary but aid and abet the aim of the building. Every detail has been designed by one team of architects and this gives it a rare consistency and fluency.

With this recent addition ends the long list of distinguished buildings each period contributed to the college.

Even if one is not interested in architecture the college is worth a visit. College Park, where all the summer sports events take place, relieves the academic greyness of the buildings. There are mature trees, so rare in Dublin now, and immaculate lawns. In Parliament Square one comes across a colourful selection of mini- and maxi-skirted girls, bearded pacifists and Marx-inspired youths, who are likely to come from secure backgrounds.

There are some 4,500 students at Trinity. Eight per cent of the male students live in the college itself while 2·5 per cent of the female students live in

Trinity Hall in Dublin. Its most distinguished schools are medicine, semitic languages, physics, classics, and history.

Appendix: Contents of Library

The most famous possession of the Library is the Book of Kells, often called the most beautiful book in the world. It is an illuminated script of the Gospels, written in the eighth century by monks in the Columban monastery of Iona in Scotland. Displayed in a modern extension of the old Library, the entrance to which is at the East side of the building, a different page of its inconceivably elaborate and beautiful contents is shown every day. In the long room of the Library stand busts of famous alumni of Trinity. The most remarkable ones are of Swift by Roubilliac, Dr. Patrick Delany by Van Nost, and Thomas Parnell and Dr Clements by Edward Smyth. A medieval Irish harp, which is called Brian Boru's harp, is one of the antique possessions of the library.

Opening Times

The long room of the Library and its new extension can be visited Mondays to Fridays (incl.) from 10 a.m.–4 p.m.; Saturdays, 10 a.m.–1 p.m.

The Reading Rooms are closed for part of July. For permission to read in them one should apply to the librarian. On application to the porter the examination hall and chapel can be seen, if they are not in use.

The Bank of Ireland—formerly Parliament House

The very first building Arthur Young, described when he visited Dublin was the Parliament House, now the Bank of Ireland:

'The front of the parliament-house is grand; though not so light as a more open finishing of the roof would have made it. The apartments are spacious, elegant, and convenient, much beyond that heap of confusion at Westminster, so inferior to the magnificence to be looked for in the seat of empire.'

The Parliament House was the earliest important public building of the eighteenth century. Its magnificence symbolizes the Parliament that sat in it during the eighteenth century. J. P. Mahaffy wrote that oratorial debates in the House of Parliament became far more fashionable than the concert and the play.

In 1728 Chichester House, where Parliament had sat since 1660, was declared unsafe and it was decided to ask Colonel Thomas Burgh to design a new Parliament House. Burgh generously handed over this splendid commission to Edward Lovett Pearce who was only twenty-eight years old at the time. Pearce had already toured Italy and become a member of the Burlington School. It has been suggested that Pearce's striking South Colonnade was inspired by Palladio's Villa S. Sofia and Giardini's Palais Bourbon. In 1729 the foundation stone was laid with much ceremony by William Conolly, Speaker of the House of Commons and builder of Castletown, County Kildare. Before the completion of the building in 1739, Sir Edward Lovett Pearce, who had been knighted by the Viceroy in 1732, suddenly and tragically died. Over the next seventy years Parliament House was to be expanded and altered by the most noted architects in Dublin. Pearce's imposing Ionic Piazza always remained the nucleus of these buildings which covered about one and a half acres.

Between 1785 and 1787 James Gandon added the portico on the East side to give the House of Lords a more befitting entrance. He overcame the problem of different street levels by using Corinthian pillars instead of Ionic ones as Pearce had done.

Pearce's House of Lords stands to this day. A glittering Waterford glass chandelier (1788) is the focal point of this perfectly proportioned room with its barrel vault ceiling. On the side walls hang John van Beaver's tapestries (1733) of the battle of the Boyne and the Siege of Derry, to the design of Johann van der Hagen. The original mantelpiece (1748-9) is a good example of early Irish wood carving. The Mace of the House of Commons (1765, London) is on display, while the Lord's Mace is in the National Museum now. The statues over the Westmoreland Street Portico represent Wisdom, Justice and Liberty, and were carved by Edward Smyth.

In 1787 Robert Parke added the Western quadrant with the Foster Place Portico. Unlike Gandon's plain wall which connected the House of Lords' Portico to Pearce's South front, Parke's connecting wall was an open colonnade with a niched screen set a few feet behind it.

The House of Commons does not survive. A fire in 1792 destroyed it completely. Rebuilt in an inferior way, it gave way for office rooms, when Francis Johnston adapted the building to suit the needs of the Bank of Ireland. In August 1800 Parliament held its last session in College Green, and Henry Grattan declared in the House of Commons:

'Without union of hearts identification is extinction, is dishonour, is conquest.'

A substantial number of people agreed with him, among them Lord Charlemont and the Duke of

Leinster. When the British Government sold Parliament House after the Union to the Bank of Ireland for £40,000 it was with the secret understanding that the Houses should be altered in such a way as to prevent

'their being again used upon any contingency whatever as public debating rooms.'

Fortunately the House of Lords was left untouched; it is now the Court of Proprietors.

Francis Johnston transferred the Court of Requests and the entrance to the House of Commons into the magnificent Cash Office. He also changed the exterior of the building filling in Parke's open colonnade, adding pillars to Gandon's austere walls between the East portico and the South colonnade,

La Touche Ceiling

and blocking up the door and windows on the wall behind the great colonnade. He completed his clever alterations by adding the statues of Commerce, Hibernia and Fidelity to Pearce's portico.

In 1945 the Bank of Ireland created yet another exceptionally beautiful interior by transferring one of the earliest rococo ceilings in Ireland from the La Touche Bank in Castle Street to their premises. This ceiling probably dates from before 1735 and is the first known one in Ireland to contain full human figures. Its subject is 'Venus wounded by love', the artist unknown. The beauty of this sensitive work of art must be a constant delight to the directors of the Bank of Ireland.

Opening Times

Liveried attendants conduct visitors through premises during banking hours: Monday, Tuesday, Wednesday and Friday, 10 a.m.–12.30 p.m., 1.30 p.m.–3 p.m.; Thursday, 10 a.m.–12.30 p.m., 1.30 p.m.–5 p.m. Closed on Saturdays.

St Werburghs Church

An experience not to be missed in Dublin is a visit to this old building which Maurice Craig described as 'the most gracious of all Dublin's churches'. The approach to the entrance used nowadays is a gloomy passage in No 8 Castle Street. It brings one to a little backyard in which St Werburghs' massive proportions loom up surprisingly.

History was unkind to this church, yet it owes its Georgian purity to the neglect it suffered in Victorian days after it ceased to be a viceregal chapel in 1790. In 1715 Thomas Burgh built it on the site of a pre-Norman church. A fire swept Burgh's building in 1754 and his handsome façade is all that is left of it. Above the main door on this façade is a frieze of skulls and crossbones, and hourglasses with wings and bones, an unusual *memento mori* for such a prominent place.

The church as it stands is the work of John Smyth,

who restored and in 1759 reopened it. As the parish church of the castle, attended by the viceregal household, it became fashionable. In 1767 the Royal Arms in front of the Viceregal pew, the upper gallery for schoolchildren and the organcase were added. Like in other Protestant churches many concerts of Handel's music were given in St Werburghs' after Handel's visit to Dublin in 1742. With the addition of a fine tower and spire in 1768 St Werburghs achieved perfect proportions. Unfortunately the castle authorities who suspected it of being used as a convenient spying base, had the spire declared unsafe by seven architects. It was taken down and twenty-six years later the tower followed suit.

The striking feature of the church are the large windows which escaped nineteenth-century stained glass. They flood the interior with light which brings out a soft glow on the carved woodwork throughout the church. The chancel is beautifully ornamented with stucco by Michael Maguire. The only feature which does not seem to blend into the pure and simple lines of this church is a Gothic pulpit elaborately carved by Richard Stewart for the Chapel Royal, and designed by Francis Johnston.

Lord Edward Fitzgerald is buried in the vaults under the chancel, while Major Sirr, the man who arrested him and of whose wounds he died, lies in the churchyard nearby. In the entrance hall which is not used as an entrance any more there is a sixteenth-century Fitzgerald tomb. It is said to come from the All Hallows Augustinian Priory, which stood on the ground where Trinity College is now. St Werburghs' has recently been well restored.

Opening Times
Mondays to Saturdays (incl.) 10 a.m.–4 p.m. For visit to vaults, apply to Sexton's cottage.

St Patricks Cathedral (Church of Ireland)

St Patricks Cathedral was built on the site of a pre-Norman church, associated with a holy well, by Archbishop Comyn, first Archbishop of Dublin. Legend tells of St Patrick baptizing people here, when he came through Dublin.

The cathedral stood on swampy ground in the valley of the river Poddle outside the walls of the old city. Until the Poddle was led underground sixty years ago it was often flooded when the river rose. Henri de Londres, Comyn's successor, who was on bad terms with the Dean and Chapter of Christ Church Cathedral gave St Patricks Cathedral status in 1203. Thus he launched the two cathedrals on a history of rivalry. As the Liberty of the Archbishop this district escaped city jurisdiction until 1860. It developed into terrible slums at the close of the nineteenth century and remained so until Lord Iveagh built the redbrick Iveagh Trust buildings and St Patricks Park in 1903.

The present cathedral was erected between 1220–60 but suffered much from abuse and neglect over the centuries. In the fourteenth century two fires ravaged the building, and the constant dampness from the river weakened the fabric. Renovated several times, it was not until the complete and drastic restoration, financed by Sir Benjamin Lee Guinness, that the structure of the cathedral was secured. A statue of Sir Benjamin stands near the entrance to the cathedral.

The tower on the North West side was added in the fourteenth century by Archbishop Minot, and the spire, designed by George Semple, was built in 1749. Swift had objected to the erection of a brick spire during his lifetime.

The cathedral was in turn endowed, degraded and restored. It has served as a fortress, a prison, a court of law and a college. In the sixteenth century some of its contents were ravaged by orders of Henry VIII and in the seventeenth century Cromwell is said to have used it as a stable for his soldiers' horses. In 1690 William III celebrated his victory at the Boyne in a service of thanksgiving. But it was Jonathan Swift (1667–1745), Dean of St Patricks Cathedral from 1713 to 1745, who brought fame to the cathedral.

It is built in the shape of a Latin cross with an aisled nave, transepts, a choir and an eastern, square Lady Chapel. During the eighteenth century the North transept served as a parish church of St Nicholas Without, while the South transept was used as a chapter house for centuries. The choir is the best preserved part of the medieval church. Banners hanging above the stalls are of the Order of St

Patrick, founded by George III in 1783. The order ceased to be associated with the church in 1871 after the disestablishment of the Church of Ireland. The Lady Chapel which had been given to the Huguenots from 1666 to 1816 was rebuilt between 1845–50.

Standing in the middle of the cathedral, one is over-awed by the massive areas of stone, and can well believe that this is the largest church ever built in Ireland. The Gothic starkness is softened when the wonderful sound of the organ fills the cathedral.

The Boyle monument is the most striking of numerous monuments from over eight centuries. It is a tomb of black marble and alabaster, and was erected by Richard Boyle, first Earl of Cork, in 1631, in memory of his wife Katherine Fenton. It is an elaborate renaissance screen of columns and arches in three tiers. In the central opening the figure of Sir Richard Boyle in armour lies above that of his wife in coronet and ruff and fur surcoat. Two stiff cherubs hold up stylized curtains of many folds. They are surrounded by their eleven children. One of them was Robert Boyle, the famous chemist and philosopher. The Boyle monument is the most important seventeenth century memorial in Ireland and its generous proportions astounded people at that time.

A few yards away in the North West corner of the church are two pre-Norman gravestones, supposed to come from the ancient Irish church of St Patrick.

Monuments in the North aisle include a Renaissance monument of Archbishop Thomas Jones (d. 1619), a statue of the Marquess of Buckingham by Edward Smyth (1788), a bust of John Philpot Curran and a memorial, erected by Lady Morgan to Turlough O'Carolan, the last of the Irish Bards.

The Duke of Schoenberg, who fell in the battle of the Boyne, is buried north of the altar. When his relatives did not respond to Swift's suggestion that a monument be erected in Schoenberg's honour, Swift himself put up a plain slab on which he wrote of their neglect of the Duke's memory.

The spirit of Swift has lived on and made St Patricks Cathedral a place of pilgrimage for many people. Swift's outspoken and satirical views on injustice and vice became the main part of his brilliant contribution to English literature. Many injustices in Ireland were brought to light in the secretly written and published *Drapier Letters*. Everyone knew who Drapier was, yet Swift's immense popularity among the people of Dublin protected him. It is often said that Swift went mad in his last years. He suffered, in fact, from labyrinthine vertigo in the middle ear. This was not treated at that time and caused the depression and bouts of insanity which grew worse in his old age. He died in 1745 and was buried in St Patricks Cathedral beside Stella, whom he called 'the truest, most virtuous, and valuable friend that I or perhaps any other was ever blessed with'. Many people believe that Swift was secretly married to Stella but their relationship will remain a mystery. Their tombs are in the South aisle, marked by brightly polished brass plaques, only a small distance from their epitaphs. Swift wrote his own epitaph which Yeats translated thus:

> Swift has sailed into his rest;
> Savage indignation there
> Cannot lacerate his breast
> Imitate him if you dare,
> World-besotted traveller; he
> Served human liberty.

A fine bust of Swift in Carrara marble by Patrick Cunningham, which was presented by a nephew of Swift's publisher, stands beside the epitaph.

Swift is best remembered by St Patricks Hospital, the oldest and one of the finest psychiatric hospitals in the British Isles. In his will Swift decreed that his money should go toward the foundation of a mental

The Swift Memorial

hospital. He wrote a charming little poem about his bequest:

> He gave the little wealth he had
> to build a House for Fools and Mad
> and show by one satiric touch
> no Nation wanted it so much.

Opening Times

Mondays to Fridays (incl.), 9 a.m.–6 p.m.; Saturdays, 9 a.m.–5 p.m.

With daily Morning Prayer at 10 a.m. and Evening Prayer at 5.30 p.m. (except Saturday); on Sundays, Holy Communion at 8 a.m., Morning Prayer and Holy Communion at 11.15 a.m., Evensong at 3.15 p.m.

Marsh's Library

Beside St Patricks Cathedral stands this attractive library, founded in 1703 by Narcissus Marsh who became Archbishop of Armagh. The architect was Sir William Robinson, who had been Surveyor-General of Ireland since 1661, and had built the Royal Hospital, Kilmainham in 1680. Marsh's Library is one of the few, still standing Queen Anne buildings in Dublin, and has the only interior of that time which survived and can be seen today. It was greatly assisted in its survival by being included in the extensive Guinness restoration of St Patricks Cathedral. At that time it was re-faced with stone and brick, but happily the proportions of the building and the charming interior with its fascinating contents were left untouched.

The collection of over 25,000 volumes consists of many unique early works of medicine, theology, ancient history, maps, Hebrew, Syriac, Greek, Latin

and French literature. Collections of Archbishop
Laud and Isaac Casaubon are also included in
the library. Books on display include Swift's copy
of Clarendon's *History of the Great Rebellion* with

Marsh's Library (interior)

Swift's satirical remarks pencilled in beside the text.

At the time of its foundation most of the great houses in Ireland had their own libraries, but Marsh's was the first public library in Ireland. Mahaffy's views on the reading habits of that day are interesting:

'There were great masters more than enough to show men how to read and write, and appreciate the English language; nay, the absence of slip-shod publications made the average reading much purer and better in style than it now is.'

What, in fact, did people read at that time? A summary of the chief items advertised by Swift's publisher Faulkner in *Pue* in 1741 included apart from Swift's Work in 6 vols:

Pope's *Works and Letters*
Life of Duke of Berwick
Voltaire's *Letter concerning the English nation*
Pamela, or Virtue Rewarded (a novel)
The Turkish Spy, 8 vols.
Pascal's *Thoughts*
Gib's *Architecture*
Compleat Family piece—receipts for Physics, Surgery, Cooking, Hawking, Hunting, Fishing, etc.

Opening Times
Mondays, 2–4 p.m.; Wednesdays, Thursdays and Fridays, 10.30 a.m.–12.30 p.m. and 2 p.m.–4 p.m.; Saturdays, 10.30 a.m.–12.30 p.m. The library is closed all day on Tuesdays.

Tailors Hall

Tailors Hall in Back Lane is one of the oldest buildings left in Dublin and has a colourful history. It served many purposes and was an important part of Dublin life for two centuries. It is assumed that Richard Mills—Assistant to the Master of the City Works—was the architect and that it was built in 1706. Walking along Back Lane which leads from Newgate to Nicholas Street it can easily be recognized by an imposing pedimented archway leading up to its front door. Street levels have risen considerably in this old part of Dublin and it is therefore likely that the present front door used to be one of the tall dormer windows. The central door in the basement is probably the original door. The warm red brick of the building makes a handsome contrast to the carved stone dressings, typical of early eighteenth-century building in Dublin. The shape of the hall itself is tall and long which is repeated in the four windows and gives the room its well balanced proportions. Despite the unguarded and derelict state of the building before restoration work was begun, the hall has retained its original mantelpiece of white marble, 'the gift of Christopher Neary, Master; Alexander Bell and Hugh Craig, wardens 1784'. A little balcony, once the musicians' gallery, with delicate ironwork and crowned by a canopy, still dominates the room from above. The staircase is built at the back and leads from the basement to the attic which has a number of attractive rooms.

Originally built for the Tailors Guild, it housed many other guilds like the saddlers, tanners, hosiers and butchers, who had no premises of their own. In the beginning of the eighteenth century it was the largest public room in Dublin and therefore constantly in demand not only for assemblies and meetings, but also for fashionable parties, banquets, concerts and other entertainments. Perhaps the most significant date in the past history of Tailors Hall is 1792, when the General Catholic Committee met there, to work for Catholic Emancipation. From this meeting it derived its nickname the 'Back Lane Parliament'.

Apart from the Grand Lodge of the Dublin Freemasons, the Dublin Corporation and the Williamite Society, Tailors Hall became a meeting place for the United Irishmen until they were forced to break up their meetings there. After the Tailors Guild was dissolved the Hall became the 'Tailors Endowed School' for Protestant Boys and its long and active involvement in Dublin's life came to an end. Later still it was leased to an undenominational organization, who used it for temperance meetings, Sunday School 'workmen's reading and coffee rooms'. It stayed in their hands until the Legion of Mary leased it for a few years.

After long years of sad vacation, during which the building deteriorated steadily, the Dublin Corporation finally scheduled it for Preservation in 1967. The Tailors Hall Fund was founded by several Preservation and historical societies in Dublin in order to raise money for the restoration work which is in progress. When this task has been completed Tailors Hall will not only remind us of its distinguished past, but take its place again in Dublin's life as a meeting place for organizations and individuals.

Opening Times
On completion of the restoration work Tailors Hall can be seen by visitors.

Christ Church Cathedral

South Door of Christchurch Cathedral

*(The Cathedral of the Holy Trinity,
Church of Ireland)*

Christ Church Place was the heart of Norse and medieval Dublin. Not a trace of that period can be found on the surface today, but extensive and rewarding excavations have been carried out around Christ Church for some years now. The cathedral dominates the area.

The original cathedral was founded early in the eleventh century by Sigtryg Silkbeard, King of Norse Dublin. During the Episcopate of Archbishop Laurence O'Toole, in the year 1170, Dublin was seized by Anglo-Norman invaders under Strongbow. With the co-operation of Laurence O'Toole, Strongbow and his followers began to rebuild the cathedral on generous lines. The crypt, the choirs, the choir aisles and the transepts, were erected in the following four years, and the two chapels dedicated. Of Strongbow's period some fine Romanesque transepts and arches remain with the characteristic chevron of zig-zag mouldings. The nave is a marvellous example of Gothic architecture in Ireland. The North wall dates from 1230, leaning outwards some 12 inches from the perpendicular. In the middle of the sixteenth century the foundations moved on the sloping hill and the arched stone roof fell into the nave, destroying the South side and much of the interior. The present South side—a copy of the North side—is by George E. Street. He restored the whole cathedral in 1871–78 at the expense of the distiller, Henry Roe. The choir and the chapels were also rebuilt in the fourteenth-century style.

Street was one of the best Gothic revivalists, and the interior of Christ Church is a sensitive restoration of the original medieval church. The exterior with its flying buttresses and covered bridge leading over the road to the Synod House, which was also contributed by Henry Roe, looks stilted in character. The medieval feeling is lost in the confusing and heavy exterior.

On the South side of the nave is Strongbow's monument. There is no doubt that Strongbow is buried in the cathedral he helped to rebuild. It is, however, unlikely that this is the tomb originally erected in his memory. The latter was destroyed in the sixteenth century during the collapse of the South wall. The present effigy bears the arms of the FitzOsberts of Drogheda, from where it was transferred to Christ Church by the Lord Deputy, Sir Philip Sidney. It was important to have a 'Strongbow's Tomb' in Christ Church, as it was often entered in leases and deeds as the location for the transfer of money.

There are several theories as to what the smaller recumbent figure by its side is. One theory claims it is the original effigy of Strongbow's son, which was also severely damaged by the fall of the roof and later trimmed by a stone mason. Another theory explains its small size with a doubtful story about Strongbow cutting his son in half for showing cowardice in the battlefield. Some people think it is the figure of a woman, and some that it is a visceral monument commemorating the burial of Strongbow's bowels in Dublin.

In the South Transept the monument to the nineteenth Earl of Kildare by Sir Henry Cheere introduces an unexpected feeling of the eighteenth century. The Earl in white marble lies on a black marble sarcophagus. At his head his mourning widow is supported by a daughter, while at his feet his son advances in a dancing position, hands eloquently clasped. A rhythmical composition of great elegance and beauty.

The vaulted crypt is the most fascinating feature of the church. It dates from the twelfth century, when Strongbow and St Laurence O'Toole rebuilt the church, and therefore indicates its original size. It has a nave, with aisles and apse, and three square-ended eastern chapels. In the Middle Ages church services were held in the crypt. Later parts of it were rented by shopkeepers whose shops could be entered through doors opening into St John's Lane and the Churchyard. Until the middle of the nineteenth century it served as a place of burial. One of the most beautiful monuments in the crypt is the one of Nathaniel Sneyd by the famous sculptor Kirk. There are also statues of James II and Charles II, removed from the old 'Tholsel', or city hall, and the tabernacle and candlesticks, used when Mass was celebrated in the cathedral for the visit of James II.

The Ancient Stocks of the old 'Liberty' of the cathedral which were made in 1670 also stand in the crypt. The Dean punished offenders from within this district by making them sit in these stocks in public. Down to the eighteenth century they used to stand at the corner of Christ Church.

Christ Church was regarded as the 'State Church', or principal Chapel Royal of Ireland from its earliest days. Down to the sixteenth century the Lord Lieutenant and high Civic authorities were sworn into office here. Four Irish chieftains—O'Neill, O'Connor, O'Brien and MacMurrough—who submitted to Richard II of England, were knighted by him in the cathedral in 1395. In 1487 Lambert Simnel, the Yorkist pretender, crowned himself King Edward VI there.

It is now the Church of Ireland diocesan cathedral of Dublin and Glendalough.

Opening Times

May–September, Mondays–Saturdays (incl.), 9.30 a.m.–5 p.m.; October–April, Mondays–Saturdays, 9.30 a.m.–4 p.m. Parties are conducted around from 10.30 a.m. Choral services at 10 a.m. and 6 p.m., Mondays–Fridays (incl.). Sundays, Matins and Sung Eucharist at 11 a.m.; Evensong 3.30 p.m.

James Joyce

The James Joyce Museum, Sandycove *(No 8 bus)*

Any attempt to describe the character of Dublin must seem clumsy and inadequate when compared with what James Joyce wrote about the city sixty-five years ago. In *Ulysses*, the story of Leopold Bloom's wanderings around Dublin, he brilliantly brought it to life without a trace of sentimentality. He delighted in all the little inconsequential things that make Dublin exciting, yet might never be seen by an insensitive eye. He understood that it was impossible to define the elusive character of Dublin. Instead he subtly allowed it to speak for itself.

Joyce once told a friend:

> 'There was an English Queen who said that when she died the word "Calais" would be written on her heart. "Dublin" will be found on mine.'

It is this absolute love for Dublin which allowed him to be totally honest and uncompromising in the immortal picture he drew of it. He boasted himself that if Dublin was ever destroyed it could be faithfully reconstructed from his books. Sadly, old parts of Dublin are disappearing fast. If the erratic town planning of the city is allowed to proceed on present lines, Joyce's statement may yet have to be considered.

No 7 Eccles Street, Leopold Bloom's house, was demolished in 1967, but many of the shops, pubs, and corners Joyce so faithfully recorded in *Ulysses*, are still standing.

'Monto', the nightlife district with brothels and dubious establishments, frequented by Joyce and his friend Gogarty in their youth, has largely disappeared. Later, as a fashionable doctor in Dublin,

75

Gogarty lamented the 'passing of the kips' in a ballad.

The most interesting place for a Joyce pilgrimage is the Martello Tower in Sandycove. It was opened as a Joyce Museum on Bloomsday, 16 June 1962, by the late Miss Sylvia Beach, who first published *Ulysses*.

Early in the nineteenth century these stone fortresses were built around the coast of Ireland as a defense against a possible Napoleonic invasion. Built of hewn granite they were about 40 feet in diameter and absolutely circular and the walls were 9 feet thick.

In 1904 James Joyce lived in the Martello Tower in Sandycove for a short time with Oliver Gogarty and described it in the opening scene of *Ulysses*. They paid £8 a year rent to the British Secretary of State of War. The receipt is preserved, along with many other documents in the 'Gloomy domed living-room' of *Ulysses*. There are a few first editions,

James Joyce Museum, Sandycove

manuscripts, photographs and other personal mementoes like his walking stick and his guitar. Also there is his death mask.

In his *Rambles in Erin* Mr William Bulfin wrote about a visit to the Martello Tower, where he met Joyce and Gogarty one Sunday morning in 1904:

'... The poet was a wayward kind of genius, who talked in a captivating manner, with a keen grim humour ... The other poet listened in silence, and when we went on the roof he disposed himself restfully to drink in the glory of the sunshine ... We looked northward to where the lazy smoke lay on the Liffey's banks, and southward, over the roofs and gardens and parks to the grey peak of Killiney, and then westward and inland to the blue mountains.'

One can still climb on the roof and enjoy this view.

Opening Times
May to end of September, Mondays–Saturdays, 10 a.m.–1 p.m. and 2.15 p.m.–5.30 p.m.; Sundays, 2 p.m.–5 p.m.

Halfpenny Bridge

Tour of the North Side

The Four Courts

One of Dublin's great architectural gems is the Four Courts. Its magnificent scale as well as refinement of architectural detail, its setting on the Liffey with the quays and handsome stone bridges, all add to its attraction. The building dominates the North side of the river with much grace and no effort.

Yet it gave the architect James Gandon a lot of headaches during the period of construction between 1786 and 1802. He was constantly attacked on grounds of extravagance and money was only reluctantly advanced by Parliament. An enemy of Gandon's wrote about the 'contemptible Vanity' of the lawyers having 'the grandest building in Europe, in the World, to plead in and to walk around . . .' In the end the Four Courts were completed for about £200,000. James Gandon, who was an Englishman, has been called the master of Georgian architects in Dublin. He had been a pupil of Sir William Chambers before John Beresford brought him to Ireland in 1781, when he commissioned him to build the new Custom House. Gandon's portrait in the National Gallery by Tilly Kettle and William Cuming shows him standing in front of Dublin's sky-line with the Four Courts, the dome of the Rotunda Hospital and the Custom House, all designed by him, and holding the plans of the Four Courts.

Gandon imaginatively used a section of the Four

Courts, the Public Offices, which had been built by Cooley before he died, as a wing for the central block. He connected this with beautiful arches, and duplicated the scheme on the East side, thus achieving the colossal Palladian front.

The Four Courts

The whole complex of buildings—many of them added in the nineteenth and twentieth centuries—is dominated by the dome which was rebuilt after its destruction in 1922, when Pro-Treaty troops attacked Anti Treaty Forces, who had seized the building. The interior of the central block—the Law Library and the Public Record Office with its priceless archives—was also destroyed. The interior was rebuilt more or less on the original plans and one can still see the entrances to the four courts: the Courts of Chancery, King's Bench, Exchequer and Common Pleas. The building now houses the Supreme Court and the High Court of the Republic. The traditional uniform of wig and gown was retained, but unlike English barristers, Irish barristers do not have chambers. The Law Library is the centre of their profession.

The figure of Moses holding the tables of law crowns the pediment with Justice and Mercy by his side, and Wisdom and Authority seated on the corners. They were all carved by Edward Smyth in 1792.

Opening Times

The domed Hall can be seen Mondays to Fridays (incl.) 9 a.m.–5 p.m. Closed on Saturdays and Sundays.

St Michans

Carving on Organ Gallery

St Michans is worth a visit for many reasons, the least of them being that one can shake hands with mummified corpses in the grisly vaults.

The original St Michans dates from 1096, when it was built as the parish church for the Norse in the suburb of Oxmantown. It was rebuilt in 1685–86 by the Rector, Dr John Pooley; the interior underwent a restoration in 1828. On the West side of the church there is a beautiful doorway left from the seventeenth century; the tower is likely to date from the medieval structure.

Inside the most striking feature is an early eighteenth-century organ which Handel is said to have played during his visit to Dublin. There is a marvellous carved panel with musical instruments on the gallery in front of the organ attributed to Cuvilliès.

The only Stool of Repentance left in Dublin stands in the North East corner. A recumbent effigy of a bishop is all that remains of the ancient Norse Church.

The vaults are likely to date from the period of rebuilding in the seventeenth century, and it is even more likely that the corpses, proudly shown off as crusaders by the guide, are from this time too. Their long preservation is due to the fact that the moisture in the vaults is absorbed by the magnesium lime-stone of which they are built. To visit them is a spooky experience.

Apart from the macabre spectacle of tourists viewing the leathery remains of the unfortunate people laid to rest here, the cellars contain the family vaults of some well-known Anglo-Irish families. Crumbling coffins are heaped on top of each other, some of the early ones held in elaborate gold and metal work.

In the Clements vault lie the remains of the third Earl of Leitrim, a controversial figure in the Irish landlord saga of the nineteenth century. In 1878 he was murdered on the roadside on his estate in Donegal. The following description of his funeral appeared in Shane Leslie's book *Lord Mulroy's Ghost*:

'The dramatic inquest was followed by a dramatic funeral. When the hearse reached the family vault in St Michans Church, Dublin, drawn by four white-plumed horses, there were signs of a riot. A mob sprang from the underworld of Dublin and made every effort to hurl the coffin into the adjacent Liffey. Only the Police rescued the dead man and enabled him to be lowered into the Clements vault. The service was said by a relation, Archdeacon Hamilton, to the screaming responses of the mob.'

The most famous occupants of the vaults are the Sheares brothers. John and Henry Sheares were two republican barristers who played a prominent part in the movement of the United Irishmen. After the failure of the rising of 1798 and their arrest, their friends desperately tried to save them from their death sentences. But to no avail. After their execution their remains were brought to St Michans from Newgate prison nearby.

Opening Times

Mondays–Fridays (incl.), 10 a.m.–1 p.m. and 2 p.m.–5 p.m.; Saturdays, 10 a.m.–1 p.m.

No 9, Henrietta Street

This charming street, said to be named after Henrietta, Duchess of Grafton, was the first of Dublin's
great eighteenth-century residential streets. Luke
Gardiner laid it out in the 1720s and although it
only contained sixteen houses it was the centre of a
brilliant social and professional life till the Union.
Two years before the Union the following people
lived there:

7 peers
1 judge
2 members of Parliament
1 bishop
2 rectors
1 doctor
1 publican

Most of the houses have become slum tenements,
but Nos 9 and 10 house the Sisters of Charity of St
Vincent de Paul. Their charitable work includes
running a hostel for girls working in the city, a day
nursery for small children and a food centre as well
as some welfare visiting.

Thomas Carter, Master of the Rolls, purchased
No 9, which was probably built by Richard Castle in
1731. In 1796 it was acquired by Lord O'Neill,
who died two years later of a wound received in the
Rebellion of 1798. After his death Arthur Moore,

Justice of the Common Pleas, lived in No 9 for many years. He was known as 'Judy Moore' as he always wore his robes on his travels in order to impress people. Eventually the house was used as Barristers' Chambers, later still let in tenements until the Sisters of Charity took it over in 1898.

The staircase hall is a perfect example of compartmented walls and ceilings, the earliest type of plaster-decoration in the eighteenth century. Walls and ceilings in many houses were decorated with broad bands of plaster which form geometrical compartments. It is rigid, untouched as yet by the spontaneous profusion of rococo craftsmanship. There is also a fine stone staircase in two flights with a beautiful hammered iron balustrade.

In 1730 Luke Gardiner built No 10 for himself; it is likely that Richard Castle designed this house too. It became Mountjoy House when the Gardiners received the title of Viscount Mountjoy in 1794. The second Viscount Mountjoy was created Earl of Blessington in 1816. When his first wife died in 1814 'a room was fitted up in which the body lay in state under a pall of black velvet embroidered with gold, the coffin surrounded with candles and watched by six female mourners'. Four years later Lord Blessington married Marguerita, the famous Lady Blessington, whom he introduced to his friends in Dublin at a large dinner party in Henrietta Street.

Between 1725 and 1794 four successive Primates lived opposite Nos 9 and 10, where the King's Inns Library stands now. Of these Archbishop Stone was the most powerful character. Richard Cumberland wrote in his memoirs: 'Nothing that I had seen in England, could rival the Polish magnificence of Primate Stone, or the Parisian Luxury of Mr Clements.' The Right Hon. Nathaniel Clements, Teller of Exchequer, lived in No 7.

At the top of the street behind a beautiful curved screen lies the King's Inns, the educational and social buildings of the barristers or the advocates branches of the Irish legal profession. It was Gandon's last building, begun in 1795 with several additions being made later. His great dining hall survives to this day and can be seen on application,

Henrietta Street was one of Dublin's most beautiful streets and despite the deterioration of most of its houses and its tattered appearance, it still is beautiful.

Opening Times at No 9

The Sisters of Charity of St Vincent de Paul have kindly given permission that on weekdays, and at reasonable hours, visitors can see the interior of No 9.

No 20, Lower Dominick Street, Dominican Boys' Home

It is difficult to imagine Dominick Street as an elegant street in the eighteenth century. No 20 was one of the first houses to be built there and is now one of the few that have survived the drastic re-planning of the street. Most of the old houses gave way to modern blocks of flats. The large four bay house is the last in the row of Georgian houses and stands on the same side as the Dominican Church.

Robert West built it for himself in 1755 but leased it to the Beresford family that same year. West, who was strongly influenced by Barthelemy Cramillion at this time, put all his imagination and skill into the superb plaster decoration of this house. Like in his other work, birds are his main motif along with flowers, fruit, foliage and musical trophies. The plasterwork in the hall is breathtakingly beautiful. Executed in the highest relief it is bold to the point of asymmetry, yet absolutely controlled and submitting to the proportions of the hall.

In the drawing room downstairs and the room

above it which has been turned into a chapel, the plasterwork is light and playful. Along with familiar West motives there are charming busts of girls in the lace bodices of the century in the first room. The centre-piece of the chapel ceiling shows children at play. The chapel is lovely in its simplicity, uncluttered and comfortable.

Beside it there is another smaller room, the Venus room, with Venus resting on a dolphin on a rock in the centre ceiling. She can watch the boys of the Dominican Home play billiards; they eat and study in the drawing room below.

Originally founded in 1780, St Saviour's Orphanage—as it was called until recently—moved into No 20 in 1927. In 1964 Father McCormack was appointed to become its resident guardian, taking over full control of the Home. When they are not at school or study some of the forty-six boys—aged between eight and sixteen—often welcome visitors to look at the plasterwork which is in excellent condition. The past and present seem to be in perfect harmony in this house.

Father McCormack has very kindly given permission to visit this house at reasonable hours.

The Rotunda Hospital (Chapel)

The famous Rotunda Hospital is said to be the
oldest maternity hospital in the British Isles.
Bartholomew Mosse, a young and idealistic doctor
in Dublin was appalled by the miserable conditions
in which the poor women in Dublin had to give
birth to their children. He founded the Lying-in
Hospital in 1745. After an initial period in a house
in George's Lane, Mosse took a lease of the plot at
the northern end of Sackville Street and built the
new Lying-in hospital between 1751–57. His friend
Richard Castle, who died just before the building
was begun, had designed it without charging a fee.
John Ensor carried out the work after his death. It
bears a certain likeness to Leinster House which
Castle had finished only a few years earlier. Originally the cupola on the tower above the heavy granite
building was surmounted by a charming gilt cradle,
crown and ball.

Mosse's kind and charitable character was
matched by an extraordinary administrative ability

Plasterwork in The Rotunda Chapel

and a great love for the arts. In order to raise funds for the hospital Mosse laid out gardens at the rear of the hospital which became the scene for fashionable Dublin. There were walks, an amphitheatre, an 'orchestra' for music and pretty temples. After Mosse's untimely death in 1759 the Rotunda Assembly rooms were added by John Ensor in 1764. In 1786 Gandon improved the Rotunda, enriching it with a frieze and coade stones by Edward Smyth. The New Assembly Rooms were added later by Richard Johnston, elder brother of Francis Johnston.

In the Rotunda Assembly Rooms brilliant and diverse entertainments were given that ranged from concerts by Franz Liszt to Newman's University Discourses.

Now the Rotunda itself is the Ambassador Cinema, the Gate Theatre is housed in part of the Assembly Rooms. The Gate was founded by the late Longford and is famous for its artistic quality under the direction of Hilton Edwards and Michael MacLiammoir.

Eventually the beautiful gardens which had been compared to Vauxhall were destroyed when a red brick home for nurses was built. Most of the fine buildings in the Rotunda complex suffered unkind alterations in recent times.

But the Rotunda Chapel is still preserved in its original splendour and opulence. It is said to be the purest baroque outside of the continent. Mosse commissioned a Frenchman, Barthélémy Cramillion to decorate the chapel and paid him 500 guineas for it. Mosse's proposed plan to fill in the blank compartments of the ceilings with paintings by Cipriani was not carried out after his death. In his book *Dublin 1660–1880* Maurice Craig eloquently describes the chapel:

'It is a square of eighty-six feet, thirty feet high, occupying the whole centre of the front above the Hall. Its ceiling is without parallel in Ireland, and would be hard to match much nearer than Germany—a full-blooded baroque treatment with figures in whole relief, cherubs, terms, bunches of grapes and ribbands of text flying out from the cove.'

Leaflets with a more detailed description of the plasterwork are available in the chapel.

Opening Times
Due to the courtesy of the Hospital authorities the chapel can be visited at reasonable times. To enter it one should push open the front door (there is no bell to ring) and mount the stairs straight ahead— the Chapel is situated over the front hall. Groups are not allowed to visit the chapel.

The Municipal Gallery—formerly Charlemont House

'Charlemont House,' writes Malton in 1794, 'the town residence of the Earl of Charlemont, is most cheerfully situated on a rising ground in the centre of a well-built row of houses called Palace Row, forming the Northside of an elegant square named Rutland Square.'

The interior has been changed completely since the three-storey mansion was built in 1761–63 by Charlemont to the design of his friend Sir William Chambers. The oval staircase and the small front drawing room are the only surviving features of the eighteenth century. As Charlemont, however, became the great patron of arts and was well known to have brought back great works of art from extensive travels in his youth, it is worth reading Arthur Young's account of the interior:

'It is equally elegant and convenient, the apartments large, handsome, and well disposed, con-
taining some good pictures, particularly one by
Rembrandt of Judas throwing the money on the
floor, with a strong expression of guilt and re-
morse; the whole group fine. In the same room is
a portrait of Caesar Borgia by Titian. The library
is a most elegant apartment of about 40 by 30 feet,
and of such height as to form a pleasing propor-
tion; the light is well managed, coming in from
the cove of the ceiling, and has an exceeding good
effect; at one end is a pretty ante-room, with a
fine copy of the Venus Medici, and the other two
small rooms, one a cabinet of pictures and anti-
quities, the other medals.'

Many other visitors, who obtained an introduc-
tion to Lord Charlemont, praised the beauty of his
house and its contents. As well as being an aesthete
who closely supervised every detail of his houses
while they were built and decorated he was a patriot
and conscientious politician. He took his seat in the
House of Lords in 1754, at the age of twenty-six,
and later became Commander-in-Chief of the Irish
Volunteers. He is said to have 'had personal qualities of a kind which often go further in politics than
great brilliancy of intellect; and he was one of the
very few Irish politicians who had never stooped to
any corrupt traffic with the government'. The
'Volunteer Earl', who suffered from ill health in his
later years, died in Charlemont House in August
1799.
In 1876 the house was sold to the government by
the third Earl of Charlemont, and from that time
served as a General Register Office.
In 1930 it was altered completely when it became
the Municipal Gallery of Modern Art. The façade

97

lost by the addition of the modern front porch. The treasures inside must pacify anybody who bemoans the loss of Charlemont's magnificent interior. Outstanding among these are the Lane Pictures, a wonderful collection of impressionist and modern paintings. Sir Hugh Lane who was drowned when the *Lusitania* sank, left them to Dublin in a codicil to his will. This codicil was unwitnessed and therefore invalid. After a long legal battle between the English and Irish authorities it was agreed the collection should be divided into two parts and shown in Dublin and London alternatively in five-year cycles.

Of the Impressionists there are particularly important and beautiful works by Corot—*Palace of the Popes; Avignon*; Degas—*On the Beach*; Manet—*Concert in the Tuileries*; and Renoir—*Umbrellas*. And also Daumier, Berthe Morisot, Boudin and Monet.

Other masters represented include Constable, Turner and Whistler.

The Irish school includes besides living painters, John Butler Yeats (portrait painter) and Jack Yeats (most original and imaginative painter of Irish scenes), Orpen and Evie Hone (stained glass designer).

Of contemporary painters such names as Picasso, Segonzac, Piper and Rouault, are represented. With some sculpture by Degas, Epstein, Moore, Rodin and others.

Opening Times

Sundays, 11 a.m.–2 p.m.; Mondays, closed all day; Tuesdays, 10.30 a.m.–8 p.m.; Wednesdays–Saturdays (incl.), 10.30 a.m.–6 p.m.

The General Post Office

'Irishmen and Irishwomen: In the name of God and the dead generations from which she receives her old tradition of nationhood, Ireland, through us, summons her children to her flag and strikes for her freedom . . .'

The Proclamation of the Provisional Government of the Irish Republic to the People of Ireland started with these words, and was signed by Thomas J. Clarke, Sean Mac Diarmada, P. H. Pearse, James Connolly, Thomas Mac Donagh, Eamonn Ceannt and Joseph Plunkett. Pearse issued this proclamation from the General Post Office on Easter Monday 1916. The G.P.O. was the headquarters of the Irish Volunteers in the following week, when O'Connell Street was destroyed. Under the commands of Pearse and Connolly about 1,000 men held parts of

Cuchulain

Dublin for a week against British Forces. The General Post Office was shelled from a gunboat on the Liffey and in the end had to be evacuated by the garrison when a fire broke out.

After the surrender fifteen leaders of the Irish Volunteers were executed. A marvellous bronze statue of the dying Cuchulain, a mythical Irish hero, stands in the General Post Office in memory of these men. It is by the Irish sculptor Oliver Sheppard.

The General Post Office was built by Francis Johnston in 1814. The exterior with its Ionic portico did not suffer any serious damage during Easter Week 1916; the interior has been rebuilt since. The pediment is surmounted by statues representing Hibernia, Mercury and Fidelity.

The General Post Office stands serene and dignified in this confusing street of ice-cream parlours and cinemas, which used to be Sackville Street, one of the most elegant residential streets in the eighteenth century.

Opening Times
   Monday–Saturday (incl.), 8 a.m.–11 p.m.; Sunday, 9 a.m.–11 p.m.

101

The Pro-Cathedral

Tucked away in Marlborough Street which runs parallel to O'Connell Street, stands St Mary's Catholic Pro-Cathedral. In 1816 the amateur architect John Sweetman to whom no other work is attributed, built this Greek Revival building here after Protestant circles had objected to its erection in O'Connell Street. It is surprising that no Catholic cathedral has since been built in a more prominent place in Dublin. The massive portico of six Doric columns is said to have been copied from the Temple of Theseus in Athens. The striking white marble altar is by Turnerelli. Unlike most of the Protestant churches the Pro-Cathedral is never empty.

Other well-known Catholic churches include St Paul's Church, Arran Quay—by Patrick Byrne

1835–37, which has a beautiful tower and cupola; the very fine Jesuit Church in Upper Gardiner Street—by T. B. Keane 1832; St Andrew's, Westland Row by James Boulger 1832–37; and St Audoen's by Patrick Byrne, 1841–46, which seems the most beautiful and dignified of them all.

Opening Times

Masses in the Pro-Cathedral are held as follows: Sundays, 6.30 a.m.–12 noon, High Mass 12.35 p.m., evening Mass 5.45 p.m. and 7 p.m.; Holy Days, 6.30 a.m.–12.35 p.m., evening Mass at 5.45 p.m. and 7 p.m.; Weekdays, 7 a.m.–11 a.m., evening Mass 5.45 p.m.

The Abbey Theatre

View of the back stage

'John Synge, I and Augusta Gregory thought
All that we did, all that we said or sang
Must come from contact with the soil, from that
Contact everything Antaeus-like grew strong.
We three alone in modern times had brought
Everything down to that sole test again,
Dream of the noble and the beggar-man.'

W. B. Yeats, and Lady Gregory, John M. Synge, Edward Martyn and the Fay brothers, were the founders of the Abbey Theatre, their ideals the foundation stones. They longed for a stage on which Irish poetic drama could live, and this they achieved in spite of the tremendous odds against them.

In 1904 Yeats wrote:

'A generous English friend, Miss Horniman, had rearranged and in part rebuilt, at very considerable expense, the old Mechanics' Institute Theatre. We are, and must be for some time to come, contented to find our work its own reward . . ., and though this cannot go on always, we start our winter cheerfully with a capital of some forty pounds.'

Thus the world famous Abbey Theatre was born. The first play was *The Well of the Saints* by J. M. Synge, and the cast included Sara Allgood and the Fay brothers, names that have long since gone down in the history of the Abbey. Yeats would not subject his ideals for this theatre to any narrow nationalist opinions or materialistic considerations. After riots broke out during the first performances of Synge's *Playboy of the Western World*, he steadfastly refused to withdraw the play which was to become a classic in Irish theatre. Likewise, when a rowdy audience showed their dislike of Sean O'Casey's *The Plough and the Stars* in one of its early performances, he called them to order with 'You have disgraced yourselves again'.

He and Lady Gregory were not only writing plays for the Abbey and inspiring other writers, they were deeply interested in the artistic management of their theatre while at the same time struggling with the financial administration. Yeats demanded 'simplification of scenery and gesture lest they should detract from the significance of the spoken word in either verse or prose'. He wrote: 'There must be nothing unnecessary, nothing that will distract the attention, no restless mimicries of the surface of life.' This approach to acting became part of the Abbey tradition. The emblem of the Abbey Theatre is Queen Maeve and the Irish wolfhound, made from a woodcut design by Elinor Monsell.

In 1951 the original theatre was destroyed by a fire in which many fascinating documents and relics of its early history were lost.

In 1966 the new Abbey Theatre was completed, the architect was Michael Scott. While the exterior is plain and rather stark, which may be intended to merge into its uninspiring surroundings, the theatre inside is imaginative, well designed and extremely comfortable. It is built in the shape of a 'half-closed fan, where the audience sit on seats that rise towards the broad end while the play is played at the narrow end'. This is what Yeats said describing his ideal theatre.

Sitting in it and seeing one of the Abbey productions one feels a curious freedom of space, time and reality.

Productions in recent years have included plays by the following modern Irish playwrights: Paul Vincent Carroll, Louis D'Alton, M. J. Molloy,

Seamus Byrne, Walter Macken, John B. Keane, John Murphy, Brendan Behan and Brian Friel.

Opening Times
   Conducted tours of the Abbey during June, July and August starting at 3.30 p.m. For parties over 20 special tours can be arranged. For permission to see the Abbey Theatre at other times apply to the Manager.

The Abbey Theatre Auditorium

The Custom House

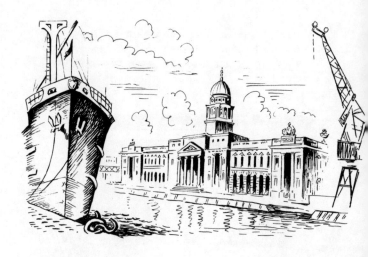

Again and again one hears the Custom House described as the most beautiful building in Dublin. Although consistent and offensive attempts were made to dwarf its greatness—in 1889 a railway line was laid beside it and in 1962 the skyscraper Liberty Hall went up—it has held its place as the sovereign of Dublin's buildings. It is also Gandon's masterpiece. The theory that Gandon's design was inspired by Chamber's Marino Casino is quite likely to be true as Gandon was a pupil of Sir William Chambers.

With no other building of his many projects in Dublin did Gandon come across more difficulties and stubborn opposition. Not only was the selected site an extremely hazardous one to build on, being partly flooded at high tide, but merchants and members of the Corporation who had made their investments further upstream objected to it strongly.

In July 1781 a mob fortified with whiskey and gingerbread, threatened to fill up the trenches that had been dug for the foundations. Due to the warm weather they ended up swimming in them.

One month after this episode John Beresford laid the foundation stone. He had commissioned Gandon with this great task and later was to live in the best rooms of the Custom House. It was to be ten years before the completion of the building at a cost of nearly £400,000.

Some of Gandon's better known Irish craftsmen included Henry Darley, the stonecutter, John Semple, bricklayer and rough mason and Hugh Henry, carpenter as well as an army of Dublin masons. Yet the undertaking was so big that they had to import more English workmen, of whom Gandon wrote:

> 'They were very orderly at first, but in the end more refractory than the natives, more exorbitant in their demands for increase of wages, and worse by far as to drunkenness.'

In 1921, when the Custom House held the main departments of the British government in Ireland, it was set ablaze by the Dublin brigade of the IRA. Nearly all the records were destroyed, virtually crippling British administration in Ireland. Gandon's interior was lost and was not built up again on its original lines.

But like the Four Courts the exterior of the Custom House escaped severe damage. A slender dome crowns the long river front of 375 feet. Edward Smyth carried out the remarkable stone carvings with which the Custom House is so richly decorated. The colossal figure of Commerce surmounting the dome, the magnificent Arms of Ireland with the harp, held by the Lion and the Unicorn, on the end pavilions, and the wonderful fourteen keystones of the basement storey, symbolizing the Atlantic Ocean and thirteen principal rivers of Ireland, are by him. As well as the ox-head frieze on the North front and the allegorical bas relief in the pediment with the figures of England and Ireland sitting on a shell, Neptune leading them and chasing away Famine and Despair.

The River Erne

Charles Bowden wrote in 1791—to quote just one of many enthusiastic comments about the Custom House:

> 'I have visited all the principal cities of Europe, but the new Custom House lately built here exceeds infinitely anything of the kind I have seen.'

Since the fire swept the Custom House in 1921 there is nothing to see inside. It is used for office purposes now.

The Marino Casino

This elaborate pavilion standing in the grounds of the O'Brien Institute, is the only non-functional eighteenth-century building in the care of the State. The Public Board of Works have looked after it for the last thirty years. Designed entirely by Chambers, it was built for the Volunteer Earl for 'solitude and retirement' in the grounds of his seaside villa Marino House. He came to love it so much that he lived in it much during his last years. His care over every detail is evident throughout this perfect building. Erected about 1761 it combined extremely modern and practical aspects for its day with exquisite beauty. The free standing columns serve as down-pipes inside, while the graceful urns on the roof are chimneys. The sculpture is by Wilton; Simon Vierpyl was the builder.

The interior is described by Thomas Nilton in his

Collection of Select Views from the Different Seats of the Nobility and Gentry in Ireland (1783–93):

> 'There is a Vestibule, Saloon, Boudoir, and Closet for books. There are in the attic four chambers for beds; and under the principal floor a kitchen and offices for servants, which receive light from an area surrounding the building ... It may be justly esteemed a chef d'oeuvre in architecture ...'

One is surprised to find that this building which gives the impression of a garden temple contains a house with three storeys, many rooms and large kitchens. The curved mahogany doors matching the curved wall in the hall, the fine wooden balustrade on the little winding staircase and the charming plaster shell on top of the staircase, represent just some of the unique detail of the Casino. The correspondence between Chambers and Charlemont shows that the Saloon was painted in white and blue,

with blue silk on the walls; the bedroom was hung with English India-paper.

Arthur Young praised the Casino enthusiastically as the building 'which ranks very high among the most beautiful edifices I have anywhere seen; it has much elegance, lightness, and effect, and commands a fine prospect'.

From the roof one has a wonderful view over Dublin harbour and the Dublin mountains. The basements and extensive underground passages were used as a small-arms school by the resistance.

Since Charlemont was a public spirited man who gave the people of Dublin access to his park, it seems most appropriate that his Casino should be open to the public.

Opening Times

At reasonable times, and preferably by appointment, the key for the Casino can be obtained from the caretaker, Mr Draper, who lives in the lodge of the next entrance on the road to Malahide.

Outside Dublin

The following four places—two houses and two gardens—are open to the public and can be reached in half an hour from Dublin.

Castletown and Carton are close enough to be seen in one afternoon.

The owners of all four properties are members of HITHA (Historic Irish Tourist Houses and Gardens Association under the auspices of the Irish Tourist Board to promote Houses, Castles and Gardens open to the public throughout Ireland).

For information about HITHA and about other properties in Ireland open to the public, apply to Mrs Brenda Weir, Secretary HITHA, Rookwood, Ballyboden, Dublin 14. Tel. 907359.

Castletown (Celbridge, County Kildare) *(12 miles from Dublin, via Lucan, bus No 67 to the gates)*

Castletown was built in 1722 by William Conolly, Speaker of the Irish House of Commons, to the design of the Italian Alessandro Galilei. Conolly, a self-made man, was not only the richest commoner, but more wealthy than all the Irish nobility with the exception of Lord Kildare. He consistently refused an English title and encouraged the promotion of Irish manufacture. In 1722 Perceval wrote to Bishop Berkeley who was advising his friend Conolly on the design of Castletown:

> 'You will do well to recommend to him the making use of all the marbles he can get of the production of Ireland for his chimneys, for since this house will be the finest Ireland ever saw, and by your description fit for a Prince, I would have it as it were the epitome of the Kingdom, and all

the natural rarities she afford should have a place there.'

Castletown was the first stone mansion in the Palladian style with flanking colonnades and wings in Ireland. This style was to be repeated many times, in both large and small houses. Castletown remained the most magnificent of them all due to its scale and the quality of its cut stone façade which remains white even on a rainy day.

The central block is of thirteen bays, uninterrupted by any break-front or pediment. The only decoration on the façade are the consoled window cases and surmounting frieze and cornice on the ground floor, and the alternatively segmental and triangular window pediments on the first floor. The back of Castletown repeats the front façade. Inside a passage running the whole length of the house on all three floors divides it in two. The magnificent entrance hall with its noble Italian proportions and the tall oak doors, simple wainscoting and coved ceilings are from the early period (1722). The elegant main staircase with its brass balustrade was only put in in 1759, when Lady Louisa Conolly was mistress of Castletown. In 1757, at the age of fifteen, she had married Thomas Conolly. She commissioned the Francini brothers, the Italian stuccadores, to decorate the staircase hall with baroque plasterwork. This elegant stucco incorporates family portraits and the heads of the four seasons, set in beautiful arabesques. She also created the print room, the only one left in Ireland, and the Long Gallery on the first floor. An Irish pupil of Reynolds decorated the Gallery in the Pompeian manner and two Venetian chandeliers were hung there in 1776. When Lady Louisa lay dying in 1821, she requested that a tent be erected in the park so that she could look at the house she loved so much.

Castletown contains over a hundred rooms. There are guided tours through the principal rooms downstairs, the Long Gallery and one of the bedrooms upstairs as well as the old kitchens and stables. There is a tearoom for visitors in the kitchen wing and a shop with Irish tweeds, Aran sweaters and other Irish goods beside the main staircase hall.

The Hon Desmond Guinness, President of the Irish Georgian Society, has purchased family portraits and important pieces of furniture that have always been in the house, and returned them to Castletown. The Castletown Trust bought the house with 120 acres in 1967 and it has become the headquarters of the Irish Georgian Society. Having been empty for some time before this it had suffered at the hands of vandals.

In July 1967 the house was opened to the public and became the first house in the Dublin region to open its doors to visitors—others have followed its example.

Opening Times

Wednesdays, Saturdays and Sundays, 2 p.m.–6 p.m. For parties special tours can be arranged. Entrance fees: 5/– per head, 1/– for children; 3/– per head for parties of 20 or more.

Carton, Maynooth, County Kildare *(Bus No 66 to the main gates)*

The Fitzgeralds who were created Earls of Kildare in 1316, became the most powerful family in Ireland. In 1739 Robert Fitzgerald, nineteenth Earl of Kildare, started to remodel and enlarge the seventeenth-century house to the designs of Richard Castle. In the same year the Francini brothers decorated the ceiling in the dining room, which is now the saloon. It is one of the most impressive rooms in Ireland, showing allegorical figures in full relief.

James Fitzgerald, the twentieth Earl of Kildare, became the first Duke of Leinster in 1766. He and his beautiful wife Emily, daughter of the second Duke of Richmond, moved into Carton in 1747, when the house had just been completed. He invited the famous landscape artist 'Capability Brown' to work for him in Ireland. The reply from Brown was that he 'had not finished England yet'. The park was carefully laid out on the natural lines which had just become fashionable and enclosed with a wall. Bridges and lodges were built and trees planted.

One of the children of the first Duke of Leinster and his wife Emily was Lord Edward Fitzgerald, the well-known patriot.

There are many contemporary accounts of the brilliant life at Carton in the second half of the century. A Lady Caroline Dawson, who stayed there in the autumn of 1778, gave vivid descriptions of every detail she observed:

'. . . The Duchess appears in a sack and hoop and diamonds at every meal, and such qualities of plate, etc. that one should imagine oneself in a palace; and there are servants without end.'

and in another passage:

'It is not the fashion at Carton to play at cards. The ladies sit and work, and gentlemen lollop about and go to sleep—at least the Duke does . . . I forgot to tell you the part you would like best —French horns playing at breakfast and dinner. There are all sorts of amusements; the gentlemen are out hunting and shooting all the mornings.'

In 1815 extensive alterations were carried out by the third Duke of Leinster to the design of Sir Richard Morrison, the Irish architect. He moved the approach roads and entrance to the North West side of the house so that the main rooms were facing South. Morrison's most remarkable work in the house was the addition of the stately dining room. It has an ornate plaster ceiling of the later period and two fine marble chimney pieces, one of which was moved here from Leinster House. His reading-room, now the library, is charming, with a spiral staircase leading to a little gallery which gives easy access to the books. Near the library is the beautiful Chinese bedroom which was hung with Chinese wallpaper in about 1750 and has an elaborately carved Chippendale overmantle. Queen Victoria slept in this room during her visit to Carton on 10 August 1849. The house has not been changed since she and Prince Albert saw it then.

In 1949 Carton was bought by the second Lord Brocket, who carried out extensive repairs and restoration work. His son, the Hon David Nall-Cain now lives there with his family. They opened the house to the public in July 1969.

Opening Times

House, Gardens and Shell Cottage open on Saturdays, Sundays and Bank holidays 2 p.m.–6 p.m., Easter to end of September. Admission: House and Gardens only 6/–; including Shell Cottage 8/–. Children: House and gardens only 2/–. Parties of 20 and over, Saturdays only, House, Garden and Shell Cottage 5/–; House and Garden 4/–. Teas and refreshments in the Old Kitchen and Georgian ornamental dairy. Enquiries: Tel. Dublin 286250.

Howth Castle Gardens

The Howth peninsula stretches into the sea, forming the North East boundary of Dublin Bay. It rises to over 550 feet and provides a breathtaking panoramic view over Dublin and its surrounds. In his book *Joan and Peter* H. G. Wells gave the following description of the view from the hill:

'They stood in the midst of one of the most beautiful views in the world. Northward they looked over Ireland's Eye at Lambay and the blue Mourne Mountains far away: westward was the lush green of Meath, southward was the long reach of the bay sweeping round by Dublin to Dalkey, backed by more blue mountains that ran out eastward to the Sugar Loaf. Below their feet the pale Castle clustered amidst its rich greenery, and to the East the level blue sea.'

The history of the castle must invariably interest the visitor who comes to see the gardens.

122

The present castle dates from the fourteenth century, when it was built on the site of an earlier wooden fortress, with many additions being made every hundred years in the following centuries. In 1910 the last renovation was undertaken by the architect, Sir Edwin Lutyens.

The St Lawrence family have lived on the hill of Howth since the twelfth century. Almeric Tristam commanded John de Courcy's forces, which landed at Howth in 1177. He is said to have made a vow that he would take the name of St Lawrence, if he won the battle of Howth which took place on the Feast of St Lawrence.

In 1909, on the death of William, fourth Earl and thirty-first Lord of Howth, the male line of the St Lawrence family became extinct. The estates passed on to a nephew, Julian Gaisford, who assumed by royal licence the arms and name of St Lawrence. The present owner, who lives with his family in the castle, is Captain Christopher Gaisford St Lawrence, thirty-fourth successor to Almeric Tristam.

A famous legend about Grainne Ni Mhaille, proud Queen of the West, is associated with the castle. In 1591 she returned with her fleet from England where she had been received by Elizabeth I. She asked for hospitality from Lord Howth and was refused. Her revenge for this insult was to kidnap the heir, returning him on condition that the Gates should be left open and an extra place laid for her and the head of the O'Malley family forever. She put a curse on the heir, should this tradition not be observed. It has been kept to this day.

The Gardens are well known for the Beech Hedge Walk and the rhododendrons. The hedges are over 30 feet high and in all over half a mile long. They were planted early in the eighteenth century and have been constantly clipped ever since. It takes one man four months to clip them.

The famous rhododendron plantations are situated about half a mile from the castle, growing almost vertically on the cliff. In the middle of the nineteenth century the thirtieth Lord Howth planted rhododendrons, having peat carried to the bare cliff face in buckets and placed between rocks. Originally, plantings were mainly the common purple *Rhododendron Ponticum*, but later innumerable varieties were planted in its stead.

The collection of rhododendrons now numbers about 2,000 different species and hybrids. These thrive in this ideal situation. It provides them with peaty soil, humid air, a mild climate and protection from the wind by the conifers and birches that were planted on the open clearings in between.

The gardens are at their best in May and June. However, the position of the Howth Desmesne and the unique view over Dublin and the sea, make a visit well worth while at any time, when the gardens are open.

Opening Times
   Easter to 15 September daily 11 a.m.–6 p.m.; except April 11 a.m.–2.30 p.m.; except May/June 11 a.m.–9 p.m. Entrance fees: Adults 2/–, Children 6d, Cars 2/–.

Powerscourt Gardens, Enniskerry, County Wicklow *(14 miles from Dublin)*

During the reign of Edward I Powerscourt was a royal castle, held by Eustace le Poer, from whom it derived its name. Shortly afterwards it was taken over by the O'Tooles, who were in possession of it for two centuries. In 1603 King James I granted the desmesne to Sir Richard Wingfield who eventually became Knight-Marshal of Ireland, and was later given the rank of Viscount.

Richard Castle built the present house in 1730, incorporating the original castle. In 1881 the East and West wings flanking the main block were added and other changes undertaken.

In 1961 the House and estate of about 14,000 acres were purchased from the ninth Viscount Powerscourt by Mr and Mrs R. C. G. Slazenger.

Powerscourt is famous for its formal, terraced gardens which slope gently into the landscape of

Wicklow, crowned in the distance by the Sugar Loaf Mountain. To reach the gardens one enters through the Eagle Gates. A long avenue lined with magnificent beech trees which were planted 200 years ago, brings one past the house and yards to the Bamberg Gate, the entrance to the Gardens. This Gate has a three-dimensional effect often used in churches in Bavaria where it came from.

On the way to the terraces one passes a memorial to Julia, widow of the seventh Viscount, which was erected by her son in 1931. It is adorned with busts of the four great Italian Masters: Michelangelo, Leonardo da Vinci, Benvenuto Cellini and Raphael. They stand on marble pedestals and look over a delightful, cool lily pond. Opposite Julia's Memorial is the exquisite Venetian Gate which has a vine leaf pattern. It was made by Moïse della Toure in Venice. Like the Bamberg Gate it was brought to Ireland by the seventh Viscount Powerscourt. Proceeding along the walk through the attractive Chorus Gate one comes to the terraced gardens. They were laid out by the sixth Viscount between 1843–75 to the design of Daniel Robertson. The latter is said to have given orders from a wheelbarrow, in which he was wheeled about, too drunk to walk. One hundred men with horses and carts created this unique piece of landscape gardening which gave good employment during the lean years of the famine.

The terraces are decorated with much statuary and ironwork brought from Italy and Germany by the Viscounts Powerscourt. Outstanding among these are the two bronze Pegasi, or winged horses which stand at the foot of the terraces and look striking against the silvery waters of the lake. They are the heraldic supporters of the Wingfield coat of arms. In the centre of the lake the Triton Fountain throws a jet of water to a height of about one hundred feet.

Many rare species of trees have been carefully planted in the park over the last two hundred years. They include an Araucaria Cunninghami (one of the Monkey Puzzle Family) which is said to be the only one of its kind in Europe; and a Sitka Spruce, the tallest in the British Isles, rising to over 200 feet; as well as a number of Eucalyptus Trees, planted in 1898. There is also a Japanese Garden with a good variety of exotic shrubs. A rhododendron drive through the Estate leads to the Powerscourt Waterfall, the highest in Ireland, cascading 400 feet down the black rock.

Opening Times

Estate and Gardens (Easter–October), 10.30 a.m.–5.30 p.m. Adults 4/–; Children under fourteen years 2/–; Reduction for parties over twenty in number. Conducted half-hourly tours Sundays and Bank Holidays, 2 p.m.–5 p.m. Café and Souvenir Shop. Pot plants and seasonal fruit for sale. Waterfall (open all year), 10 a.m.–7 p.m. Adults 1/–; Children under fourteen years 6d; Cars and motor cycles 1/–.